Cookies

CYNTHIA SCHEER
Writer and Food Stylist

JANET KESSEL FLETCHER
Contributing Writer

BARBARA FELLER-ROTH
Editor

MICHAEL LAMOTTE
Photographer

SARA SLAVIN
Photographic Stylist

CALIFORNIA
◇ CULINARY ◇
ACADEMY

Cynthia Scheer is a San Francisco area based food writer and home economist whose interest in baking began with her first job at the Wheat Flour Institute, a Chicago trade association devoted to encouraging home baking. She has been a magazine food editor, and has written 17 cookbooks on a variety of subjects. Her other books in the California Culinary Academy series are *Breads, Breakfasts & Brunches, Soups & Stews, Affordable Elegant Meals,* and *Salads.* She has traveled extensively throughout the United States, Mexico, and Europe to explore and experience the foods of different regions. **Janet Kessel Fletcher** is a freelance food and wine writer and editor. She holds a degree in economics from Stanford University and attended the Culinary Institute of America in Hyde Park, New York. She has worked as a professional baker in the Catskills and in San Francisco and has cooked in several West Coast restaurants, including the highly acclaimed Chez Panisse. She now writes a weekly restaurant column for the Oakland *Tribune* and produces newsletters, brochures, and promotional literature for clients in the food and wine industry.

The California Culinary Academy In the forefront of American institutions leading the culinary renaissance in this country, the California Culinary Academy in San Francisco has gained a reputation as one of the most outstanding professional chef training schools in the world. With a teaching staff recruited from the best restaurants of Western Europe, the Academy educates students from around the world in the preparation of classical cuisine. The recipes in this book were created in consultation with the chefs of the Academy. For information about the Academy, write the Office of the Dean, California Culinary Academy, 625 Polk Street, San Francisco, CA 94102.

Front Cover

This tempting collection of cookies hints at the variety to be found in the pages ahead. Sample candy-sprinkled Spritz (page 115), pinwheel refrigerator cookies (page 84), apricot-filled Little Rascals (page 100), Bite-Sized Lemon Tarts (page 71), and sugar-coated Cinnamon Balls (page 61), as well as Spiced Peanut Cookies in the jar (page 23).

Title Page

Buttery Traditional Sugar-Cookie Cutouts (page 92) are suitable for just about any holiday the year around.

Back Cover

Upper Left: Crunchy nut meringue Cinnamon Stars (page 107) bring sparkle to a Christmas table.

Upper Right: Sugar-dusted Fresh Lemon Bars (page 43) are elegant enough to serve with a celebratory flute of champagne.

Lower Left: Pine-Nut Crescents and Brown-Sugar Twists (both recipes are on page 69) suggest two fanciful ways to shape homemade cookies.

Lower Right: The tiniest cutter you can find is used to form diminutive Thimble Cookies (page 92) for a tea party in miniature.

Contributors

Calligraphers
Keith Carlson, Chuck Wertman

Consultants
Janet and Robert Johnson

Illustrator
Edith Allgood

Additional Photographers
Laurie Black, author and chefs, at left
Alan Copeland, Academy photography
Marshall Gordon, pages 25, 74, 99, 100, and 115

Photographer's Assistant
Bruce E. James

Additional Food Stylists
Doug Warne, pages 25, 74, 99, 100, and 115

Copy Chief
Melinda E. Levine

Editorial Coordinator
Kate Rider

Copyeditor
Judith Dunham

Indexer
Elinor Lindheimer

Proofreader
Andrea Y. Connolly

Editorial Assistance
Tamara Mallory, Raymond F. Quinton

Composition and Pagination
Linda M. Bouchard, Robert C. Miller

Production Artist
Lezlly Freier

Special Thanks to
Debra Ayerst, Kathleen and Roger Craig, Olivia Erschen, Hedy Green, Lynn Hartnett, Joan Melim, Lillian Moss, Florence Moy, Lisa Osta, Mr. and Mrs. Alex Scheer, Bob Simmons, Jim Stockton, and Karen Tucker.

Series format designed by
Linda Hinrichs, Carol Kramer

Lithographed in U.S.A. by
Webcrafters, Inc.

Separations by
Color Tech Corp.

The California Culinary Academy series is produced by the staff of Ortho Information Services.

Publisher
Robert J. Dolezal

Production Director
Ernie S. Tasaki

Series Managing Editor
Sally W. Smith

Systems Manager
Leonard D. Grotta

Address all inquiries to
Ortho Information Services
575 Market Street
San Francisco, CA 94105
Copyright © 1987
Chevron Chemical Company
All rights reserved under international and Pan-American copyright conventions.

1 2 3 4 5 6 7 8 9

87 88 89 90 91 92

ISBN 0-89721-099-9

Library of Congress Catalog Card
Number 87-070195

Chevron Chemical Company
575 Market Street, San Francisco, CA 94105

C O N T E N T S

Cookies

Even grandmother can't bake better drop cookies than Spiced Peanut Cookies on right (page 23) and crunchy Dutch Caramel-Praline Cookies on left (page 13).

Drop Cookies

Plump oatmeal cookies dimpled with raisins. Chocolate-chip cookies hot from the oven, the melted chocolate shimmering in inviting pools. Mention cookies and these are the childhood memories that spring to mind. Making drop cookies is often a child's first baking experience: stirring in raisins, dipping a finger into the batter to lick, and the seemingly endless wait as the cookies bake. Because drop cookies demand few sophisticated skills, they enjoy an anyone-can-do-it reputation. Anyone who does will be rewarded with wonderful flavors and melt-in-the-mouth textures for the slight effort involved.

CHOCOLATE COOKIES

Somewhere there are people who can take chocolate or leave it alone. But even those with such firm resolve on occasion need the reassurance of a mouthful of melting chocolate. The following cookies are one of the best ways to appease the appetite for chocolate.

You can incorporate the chocolate in a variety of forms—chips, ground, chopped, shards, cocoa, and melted. (For tips on melting chocolate successfully, see page 10.)

FAVORITE CHOCOLATE-CHIP COOKIES

One of the more trifling culinary debates concerns the texture of chocolate-chip cookies: crisp versus chewy. It's trifling because, depending on your preference, it is easy to have them both ways. Using the same butter-rich, walnut-studded dough, these cookies will be crisp if baked at the temperature specified in the main recipe, and soft and chewy if baked at the lower temperature suggested in the variation. So try them with semisweet or milk-chocolate chips, with irregular chunks of your favorite chocolate bar, with or without nuts, or using the distinctive peanut butter variation. In all their possible guises, these qualify as the most sought-after cookies of all time.

 1¼ cups flour
 ½ teaspoon baking soda
 ¼ teaspoon salt
 ½ cup butter or margarine,
    softened
 ½ cup firmly packed
    brown sugar
 ½ cup granulated sugar
 1 egg
 1 teaspoon vanilla extract
 1 package (6 oz) semisweet
    chocolate chips
 ½ cup chopped walnuts
    (optional)

1. In a bowl stir together flour, baking soda, and salt to combine thoroughly; set aside.

2. Preheat oven to 375° F. In mixer bowl combine butter and sugars; beat until fluffy and well blended. Beat in egg. Add vanilla and mix well.

3. Gradually add flour mixture until just blended. Stir in chocolate chips and walnuts (if used).

4. Drop by rounded tablespoons, placed well apart, onto lightly greased baking sheets. Bake until cookies are well browned (12 to 14 minutes). Cool on wire racks.

Makes about thirty 2¾-inch cookies.

Chewy Chocolate-Chip Cookies
Bake cookies in a 325° F oven until they are a light golden brown (10 to 13 minutes). Cool on baking sheets for 3 minutes before removing to wire racks to cool completely.

Chocolate-Chunk Cookies
Omit semisweet chocolate chips. Coarsely chop a 3- to 4-ounce bar of semisweet chocolate, and fold it into cookie dough in step 3.

Peanut Butter–Chocolate-Chip Cookies
After beating butter and sugars, add ½ cup peanut butter (smooth or chunky). Beat well, then continue as for Favorite Chocolate-Chip Cookies. Omit chopped walnuts.

CHOCOLATE-PECAN MERINGUES

Clouds of chocolate meringue perch atop clustered pecan halves to make these puffy and delicate cookies. Using sheets of baking parchment to line the baking sheets will enable you to remove the cookies intact. Look for it in cookware stores and mail-order catalogs if unavailable in the supermarket.

 72 pecan halves
 2 egg whites (¼ cup)
 ¼ teaspoon cream of tartar
 ⅛ teaspoon salt
 ⅔ cup sugar
 1 teaspoon vanilla extract
 3 tablespoons unsweetened
    cocoa

1. Place parchment paper or brown wrapping paper on baking sheets. On parchment make clusters of 3 pecans each, spacing clusters 2 inches apart. Preheat oven to 300° F.

2. In mixer bowl combine egg whites, cream of tartar, and salt. Beat at high speed until foamy. Gradually add sugar, beating until egg-white mixture is stiff and glossy.

3. Reduce speed and beat in vanilla and cocoa until cocoa is completely incorporated.

4. Drop a rounded teaspoonful of the cocoa mixture over each cluster of pecans. Bake until meringues are firm to the touch (25 to 30 minutes). Remove to wire racks to cool.

Makes 2 dozen 2-inch cookies.

SOUR-CREAM CHOCOLATE DROPS

In making these brownielike cookies, time can be saved by mixing the ingredients in the same saucepan used to melt the butter and chocolate.

 1¼ cups flour
 ½ teaspoon each baking powder,
    baking soda, and ground
    cinnamon
 ¼ teaspoon salt
 ½ cup butter or margarine
 3 squares (3 oz) unsweetened
    chocolate
 ¾ cup granulated sugar
 ½ cup firmly packed
    brown sugar
 1 egg
 1 teaspoon vanilla extract
 ½ cup sour cream
 ¾ cup chopped pecans
    Chocolate sprinkles (optional)

1. In a bowl stir together flour, baking powder, baking soda, cinnamon, and salt to combine thoroughly; set aside.

2. Preheat oven to 350° F. In a heavy, 2-quart saucepan, combine butter and chocolate. Place over low heat until both are melted, stirring occasionally.

3. Remove chocolate mixture from heat; stir in sugars. Add egg and vanilla; beat well. Add flour mixture alternately with sour cream, mixing until smooth after each addition. Stir in pecans.

4. Drop by tablespoons, about 1½ inches apart, onto lightly greased or nonstick baking sheets. Decorate with chocolate sprinkles (if desired). Bake until cookies feel firm when touched lightly (12 to 14 minutes). Cool on wire racks.

Makes about forty-two 2½-inch cookies.

A bar of delectable imported chocolate, coarsely chopped, transforms Favorite Chocolate-Chip Cookies into luxurious Chocolate-Chunk Cookies. You can bake these cookies to your taste—either crisp or chewy.

BOHEMIAN CHOCOLATE COOKIES

Meltingly tender and rich, the ground semisweet chocolate in these luscious cookies is a subtle presence. The low baking temperature—275° F—called for in this recipe accounts in part for the unusually rich texture of these fragile cookies. Be sure to let them cool a bit before removing them from the baking sheets to the wire racks so you won't break any.

> 1 cup walnut pieces
> 2 squares (2 oz) semisweet baking chocolate
> 1 cup butter or margarine, softened
> ½ cup sugar
> 1 teaspoon vanilla extract
> 1¼ cups flour

1. Whirl walnuts in food processor, using short, on-off bursts, until almost powdery (or use a nut grinder to grind finely); set aside. Whirl chocolate in food processor or blender until powdery; set aside.

2. Preheat oven to 275° F. In mixer bowl combine butter and sugar, and beat until fluffy and well blended. Add vanilla and chocolate and mix thoroughly.

3. Gradually mix in flour, then walnuts, until well combined.

4. Drop cookies by heaping teaspoons, placed slightly apart, onto ungreased baking sheets. Bake until cookies are firm and lightly browned (35 to 40 minutes). Let cookies stand on baking sheets for about 5 minutes before removing them to wire racks to finish cooling.

Makes about fifty-four 2-inch cookies.

Please a chocolate fancier with Chocolate-Pecan Meringues (left) and Sour-Cream Chocolate Drops (see page 6), or Bohemian Chocolate Cookies (bottom).

Tips

HOW TO MELT CHOCOLATE

Melting chocolate to use as a cookie ingredient or decoration requires low heat. If the chocolate is overheated, it may become grainy and hard. There are several good ways to melt chocolate so that it will be smooth and glossy. Choose the one that you find most convenient.

In a double boiler Place the chocolate, in one piece or chopped coarsely, in the top of a double boiler over simmering (not boiling) water until chocolate is shiny and liquidy. For the amount of chocolate called for in most cookie recipes, there is no need to stir the chocolate as it melts.

Over direct low heat Place the chocolate, coarsely chopped if desired, in a small, heavy pan over the lowest heat setting. On a gas range, where even the lowest flame may be too hot, the heat of the pilot light should be sufficient to melt the chocolate.

In a microwave oven Place the chocolate, coarsely chopped if desired, in a small glass bowl or measuring cup in the microwave oven. The time it takes for the chocolate to melt will vary, depending on the amount of chocolate and the wattage (cooking power output) of the oven. For example, in a 500-watt oven a 1-ounce square of chocolate melts in 2 minutes on the high power setting; a 6-ounce package of semisweet chocolate chips takes 1½ to 2 minutes to melt. To determine times, consult the instruction book for your microwave oven. If you are melting more than an ounce, stir the chocolate once—about halfway through the time indicated.

Note For most recipes, chocolate should be cooled slightly before it is used. Let chocolate stand for 5 to 10 minutes or until it is only slightly warm to the touch.

CHOCOLATE DATE-NUT DROPS

Chopped dates give these chewy chocolate drop cookies an unexpected flavor. In the fall look for fat, fresh Medjool dates to make the cookies extraspecial.

1 cup flour
½ teaspoon baking soda
⅛ teaspoon salt
¾ cup butter or margarine, softened
½ cup each granulated sugar and firmly packed brown sugar
1 egg
1 teaspoon vanilla extract
2 squares (2 oz) unsweetened chocolate, melted and cooled
1 cup each chopped pitted dates and chopped walnuts

1. In a bowl stir together flour, baking soda, and salt to combine thoroughly; set aside.

2. Preheat oven to 375° F. In mixer bowl combine butter and sugars; beat until fluffy and well blended. Beat in egg until fluffy. Add vanilla and chocolate; mix well.

3. Gradually add flour mixture until just blended. Stir in dates and walnuts.

4. Drop by slightly rounded tablespoons, placed slightly apart, onto ungreased baking sheets. Bake until tops of cookies feel firm when touched lightly (8 to 10 minutes). Let stand for a minute or two, then cool on wire racks.

Makes about 4 dozen 2½-inch cookies.

TRADITIONAL COOKIES

Some flavors bring back cherished thoughts of the cookie jars of one's childhood; the homemade cookies that accompanied a meat-loaf sandwich in a brown paper sack, just after fourth period; and the unexpected parcel, fragrant with sugar and spice, tucked into the fresh laundry sent from home during college days.

Such flavors are recalled in lemony sour-cream sugar cookies or spicy Raisin Rocks. They're still a treat today.

POPPY-SEED WAFERS

Crisp and tender, these cookies are made with salad oil. An abundance of poppy seed gives them a subtle flavor so they are satisfying without being overly sweet. They will stay crisp and taste fresh for up to a week in an airtight container.

1 cup flour
¼ teaspoon salt
¼ cup poppy seed
3 eggs, at room temperature
½ cup sugar
1 teaspoon vanilla extract
⅓ cup salad oil (such as corn or safflower)

1. In a bowl stir together flour, salt, and poppy seed to combine thoroughly; set aside.

2. Preheat oven to 350° F. In mixer bowl beat eggs at high speed until thick and light colored. Gradually beat in sugar, then vanilla. Beat in oil until well combined.

3. Gradually beat in flour mixture until smooth and well blended.

4. Drop by generous teaspoons, placed about 2 inches apart, onto well-greased baking sheets. Bake until cookies brown around edges (12 to 14 minutes). Carefully remove at once to wire racks to cool.

Makes about sixty-six 2¼-inch cookies.

TOOLS FOR BAKING COOKIES

One of the pleasures of making cookies is that they don't require lots of obscure or expensive ingredients or utensils. Nevertheless, baking will be easier and more fun if your kitchen is equipped with the basics.

Here are the most frequently used utensils for cookie baking, more or less in order of importance.

Baking sheets Shiny metal pans reflect heat and produce cookies that are delicately browned—especially important when you are making thin cookies. Dark-colored baking sheets hold heat and tend to brown cookies more deeply, giving them a crisper, heavier crust.

Baking sheets should have a flat or barely turned-up edge so that oven heat can reach every cookie evenly from all directions.

Because an even surface promotes uniform baking, it's best to buy baking sheets that are heavy enough so they won't warp readily.

Insulated baking sheets are an innovation that has solved many cookie bakers' problems. Air between the two sheets of aluminum that make up these baking sheets prevents cookies from burning on the bottom and promotes even baking. If you use an insulated baking sheet, you may find baking times increase slightly—generally requiring the maximum baking time given in the recipe.

Nonstick baking sheets are useful if they are made from heavy-gauge metal and coated with a top-quality nonstick material or silicone resin. If you care for them according to the manufacturer's directions, it shouldn't be necessary to grease them in order to bake most cookies. When removing cookies from nonstick pans, use a spatula that won't scratch the surface.

Cooling racks Level wire racks enable cookies to cool quickly and evenly, with air circulating from all directions. Their shape doesn't matter, but having enough of them is a must if you bake often. Cookies are at their best if they can cool completely before you stack and store them.

Pans for bar cookies Most of the cookies in Chapter 2 (beginning on page 31) are baked in standard square or rectangular pans. The most frequently used sizes are an 8-inch square, a 9-inch square, and a 9- by 13-inch rectangle. The same baking characteristics can be found in these pans as in baking sheets of comparable materials.

Bar cookies can also be baked in glass ovenware of the dimensions specified above. It's usually recommended that the oven temperature be lowered by 25° F when bar cookies are baked in glass ovenware.

Measuring equipment Use standard measuring spoons and measuring cups. Measure liquid in a glass or plastic measuring cup with a pouring spout and dry ingredients in nested metal or plastic cups that permit the contents to be leveled off at the rim.

Timer Many cookies bake in such a short time—10 minutes or less—that it's important to clock accurately how long they're in the oven. Set a timer so it can remind you when cookies are ready to be checked.

Spatulas Most experienced bakers find they use at least three kinds of spatulas. A narrow metal spatula is useful for leveling off dry ingredients as you measure them and for loosening the edges of bar cookies from a pan. A wide, flexible metal spatula is essential for removing cookies from baking sheets. A rubber spatula is handy for scraping ingredients from the side of a bowl or the blades of an electric mixer and for spreading bar-cookie batter in a baking pan.

Sifters and sieves Most cookies don't require sifted dry ingredients (stirring thoroughly in a bowl is sufficient). But you may find a fine sieve useful for removing lumps from confectioners' sugar or cake flour, and also for sifting a decorative coating of confectioners' sugar or cocoa over the surface of baked cookies.

Rolling pins In a pinch you can roll out cookie dough using a long, smooth bottle (such as a wine bottle). But you'll find rolling most cookies easier if you use a heavy, hardwood rolling pin with ball bearings.

Ruler A ruler in the kitchen proves surprisingly useful—for measuring the dimensions of bar cookies to be cut uniformly, the thickness of a rolled-out dough, or the diameter of a roll of refrigerator-cookie dough.

Baking parchment Parchment paper, available in rolls or sheets, helps to prevent very delicate cookies, such as meringues, from sticking to a baking pan.

Electric appliances An electric mixer on a heavy stand is so versatile that it is an invaluable tool for every kind of beating, creaming, and mixing involved in baking all kinds of cookies.

A portable electric mixer is useful for making soft cookie doughs and all kinds of cookie batters. It's also good for beating eggs and whipping cream.

A food processor does many otherwise tedious jobs, such as chopping quantities of nuts. Several recipes in this book are designed specifically for the processor.

A blender also makes quick work of chopping nuts, reducing poppy seed to a powder, or making puréed fruit fillings.

Cookie cutters To create the fancy-shaped cookies in Chapter 5 (beginning on page 91) and Chapter 6 (beginning on page 103), you will need sharp metal cutters in appropriate shapes.

LEMON SPONGE COOKIES

Resembling sponge cake in texture, these light and delicate cookies are delicious with tea. The cookies do not contain butter or other shortening.

    1   cup sifted cake flour
    1¼ teaspoons baking powder
    ⅛   teaspoon ground nutmeg
    2   eggs, at room temperature
    ½   cup sugar
    1   teaspoon grated lemon rind
    2   teaspoons lemon juice

1. In a bowl stir together flour, baking powder, and nutmeg to combine thoroughly; set aside.

2. Preheat oven to 400° F. In mixer bowl beat eggs until thick. Gradually add sugar, beating until thick and pale. Blend in lemon rind and juice.

3. Gradually add flour mixture until just blended.

4. Drop by level teaspoons about 2 inches apart onto well-greased baking sheets. Bake until edges of cookies are golden brown (4 to 5 minutes). Remove at once to wire racks to cool.

Makes about seventy-eight 2-inch cookies.

SPICY PUMPKIN COOKIES

These are good to make with pumpkin left over from a Thanksgiving pie. For a Halloween treat, drizzle them with orange-tinted confectioners' sugar icing after they cool.

    1½ cups flour
    ½   teaspoon baking powder
    1½ teaspoons pumpkin-pie spice
    ¼   teaspoon each baking soda
        and salt
    ½   cup butter or margarine,
        softened
    1⅓ cups firmly packed
        brown sugar
    1   egg
    ½   teaspoon vanilla extract
    1   cup canned pumpkin
    ½   cup each raisins and finely
        chopped walnuts

1. In a bowl stir together flour, baking powder, pumpkin-pie spice, baking soda, and salt to combine thoroughly; set aside.

2. Preheat oven to 350° F. In mixer bowl combine butter and brown sugar, and beat until well blended. Beat in egg until fluffy. Add vanilla and mix well.

3. Add flour mixture alternately with pumpkin, mixing until smooth after each addition. Stir in raisins and walnuts.

4. Drop by rounded teaspoons, placed slightly apart, onto greased baking sheets. Bake until edges brown lightly and tops feel firm when touched gently (18 to 20 minutes). Remove to wire racks to cool.

Makes about 5 dozen 2-inch cookies.

SOFT MOLASSES COOKIES

A spicy aroma spreads throughout the kitchen and beyond as these raisin-studded morsels bake. After cooling slightly, they are tantalizingly crisp on the outside but soft within.

    2   cups flour
    1   teaspoon baking powder
    ½   teaspoon each baking soda
        and ground cinnamon
    ¼   teaspoon each ground nutmeg
        and ground ginger
    ½   cup butter or margarine,
        softened
    ½   cup each sugar and
        light molasses
    1   egg
    ⅓   cup buttermilk
    1   cup raisins

1. In a bowl stir together flour, baking powder, baking soda, cinnamon, nutmeg, and ginger to combine thoroughly; set aside.

2. Preheat oven to 350° F. In mixer bowl combine butter and sugar, and beat until well blended. Add molasses and beat until fluffy. Add egg and beat well.

3. Add flour mixture alternately with buttermilk, mixing until smooth after each addition. Stir in raisins.

4. Drop by rounded teaspoons, placed about 1 inch apart, onto well-greased baking sheets. Bake until tops are firm when touched lightly and edges are brown (12 to 15 minutes). Remove at once to wire racks to cool.

Makes 5 dozen 2½-inch cookies.

RAISIN ROCKS

Named for their craggy appearance much more than for their crisp, tender texture, these quick drop cookies have an old-fashioned, wholesome quality.

    1   cup each all-purpose flour
        and whole wheat flour
    ¾   teaspoon each baking soda
        and ground cinnamon
    ¼   teaspoon ground cloves
    ⅔   cup butter or margarine,
        softened
    1   cup firmly packed
        brown sugar
    2   eggs
    ½   teaspoon vanilla extract
    1½ cups raisins
    1   cup chopped walnuts

1. In a bowl stir together flours, baking soda, cinnamon, and cloves to combine thoroughly; set aside.

2. Preheat oven to 350° F. In mixer bowl combine butter and brown sugar, and beat until fluffy and well blended. Beat in eggs, one at a time, beating until fluffy after each addition. Add vanilla and mix to blend thoroughly.

3. Gradually add flour mixture until just blended. Stir in raisins and walnuts.

4. Drop by rounded teaspoons, placed slightly apart, onto lightly greased or nonstick baking sheets. Bake until cookies feel firm when touched lightly and are brown at the edges (15 to 18 minutes). Transfer to wire racks to cool.

Makes about fifty-four 2-inch cookies.

OLD-FASHIONED SOFT SUGAR COOKIES

Nutmeg and lemon rind punctuate the familiar flavor of these tender, cakelike cookies.

  2½ cups flour
    1 teaspoon each *baking soda and ground nutmeg*
    ¼ teaspoon salt
    ½ cup butter or margarine, softened
  1½ cups sugar
    2 eggs
    ½ teaspoon each *vanilla extract and grated lemon rind*
    1 cup sour cream
       Vanilla Granulated Sugar (see page 39), optional
    ¼ cup (approximately) raisins

1. In a bowl stir together flour, baking soda, nutmeg, and salt to combine thoroughly; set aside.

2. Preheat oven to 375° F. In mixer bowl combine butter and sugar, and beat until well blended. Beat in eggs, one at a time, mixing until fluffy after each addition. Add vanilla and lemon rind and mix to blend thoroughly.

3. Add flour mixture alternately with sour cream, mixing until smooth after each addition.

4. Drop by tablespoons, placed well apart, onto well-greased baking sheets. Sprinkle each cookie lightly with Vanilla Granulated Sugar (if used). Place one or more raisins in the center of each. Bake until cookies are golden brown (12 to 14 minutes). Remove at once to wire racks to cool.

Makes about 5 dozen 2¾-inch cookies.

DUTCH CARAMEL-PRALINE COOKIES

Bits of caramelized sugar with almonds stud these rich, buttery cookies. In the Netherlands they are known as *koggetjes.*

  1¼ cups flour
    ½ teaspoon baking powder
    ¾ cup butter or margarine, softened
    ½ cup sugar
    ½ teaspoon vanilla extract
    2 tablespoons water

Caramel Praline

    ½ cup sugar
    2 tablespoons slivered almonds

1. Prepare Caramel-Praline mixture and set aside to cool and harden. Then break into pieces and place in a plastic bag. Using flat side of a wooden mallet, crush coarsely.

2. In a bowl stir together flour and baking powder; set aside.

3. Preheat oven to 325° F. In mixer bowl combine butter and sugar, and beat until fluffy and well blended. Add vanilla and mix well.

4. Add flour mixture alternately with the water, mixing until smooth after each addition. Stir in crushed Caramel Praline.

5. Drop by rounded teaspoons, placed about 2 inches apart, onto well-greased baking sheets. Bake until edges brown lightly (14 to 16 minutes). Let cookies stand on baking sheets for 2 minutes, then carefully transfer to wire racks to complete cooling.

Makes about 3 dozen 2½-inch cookies.

Caramel Praline

1. Place sugar and almonds in a small, heavy pan over medium-high heat, stirring occasionally until sugar melts and turns a pale amber color.

2. Onto a sheet of greased baking parchment or waxed paper lining a baking sheet on a wire rack, pour out caramel mixture to make about a ¼-inch-thick layer.

SESAME CRISPS

When these almost transparently thin cookies first emerge from the oven, they are too fragile to separate from the baking sheets. Let them cool enough to handle before trying to remove them to cooling racks. If the last few become too cool and stick, return the baking sheet to the oven for about 15 seconds to resoften cookies slightly.

    ½ cup sesame seed
    ⅔ cup flour
    ¼ teaspoon baking powder
    ⅛ teaspoon salt
    ½ cup butter or margarine, softened
  1⅓ cups firmly packed brown sugar
    1 egg
    1 teaspoon vanilla extract

1. Preheat oven to 325° F. Spread sesame seed in a shallow pan. Bake, stirring occasionally, until lightly toasted (6 to 8 minutes). Set aside.

2. In a bowl stir together flour, baking powder, and salt to combine thoroughly; set aside.

3. In mixer bowl combine butter and brown sugar, and beat until fluffy and well blended. Beat in egg until fluffy. Add vanilla and mix well.

4. Gradually add flour mixture until just blended. Add toasted sesame seed and stir until well combined.

5. Drop by rounded teaspoons, placed about 2 inches apart, onto greased baking sheets. Bake until cookies are lightly browned (9 to 10 minutes). Let cookies stand on baking sheets for about 1 minute, then carefully transfer to wire racks to complete cooling.

Makes about 4 dozen 3½-inch cookies.

Even better than clean laundry from home are cookies such as these Raisin Rocks (page 12) and Old-Fashioned Soft Sugar Cookies (page 13).

FRUITED COOKIES

The addition of fruit, either by way of a hint of grated citrus peel or a generous measure of actual fruit, contributes a fresh flavor to a drop-cookie batter.

These cookies keep well—if eager hands don't snatch them from the cookie jar before you can put this quality to the test.

PINEAPPLE DATE-NUT DROPS

The mingling of two fruit flavors distinguishes these chewy cookies. A lunch-box favorite, they also pack well to send away to school or camp.

- 1½ cups flour
- 1 teaspoon baking powder
- ½ teaspoon salt
- ½ cup butter or margarine, softened
- ⅔ cup firmly packed brown sugar
- ⅓ cup granulated sugar
- 1 egg
- ½ teaspoon vanilla extract
- 1 can (8 oz) crushed pineapple, well drained
- ½ teaspoon baking soda
- 1 cup chopped pitted dates
- ½ cup chopped walnuts

1. In a bowl stir together flour, baking powder, and salt to combine thoroughly; set aside.

2. Preheat oven to 350° F. In mixer bowl combine butter and sugars; beat until fluffy and well mixed; beat in egg. Add vanilla and stir to blend.

3. In a small bowl stir together pineapple and baking soda. Add to egg mixture, combining well (don't worry if mixture looks curdled).

4. Gradually add flour mixture until just blended. Stir in dates and walnuts.

5. Drop by rounded teaspoons, placed slightly apart, onto lightly greased baking sheets. Bake until cookies are golden brown (13 to 15 minutes). Cool on wire racks.

Makes about 5 dozen 2-inch cookies.

ORANGE-COCONUT COOKIES

Drizzling these crisp, chewy cookies with an orange icing makes them look fancier than they really are.

- 2 cups flour
- 1 teaspoon baking soda
- ½ teaspoon baking powder
- ¼ teaspoon salt
- ½ cup butter or margarine, softened
- ¾ cup firmly packed brown sugar
- ¾ cup granulated sugar
- 1 egg
- 1 teaspoon vanilla extract
- 1 can (6 oz) frozen orange-juice concentrate, thawed (reserve remainder for Orange Icing)
- 1 cup each flaked coconut and chopped pecans

Orange Icing

- 1 cup confectioners' sugar
- 1 tablespoon butter or margarine, softened
- 3 to 4 tablespoons frozen orange-juice concentrate, thawed

1. In a bowl stir together flour, baking soda, baking powder, and salt to combine thoroughly; set aside.

2. Preheat oven to 350° F. In mixer bowl combine butter and brown and granulated sugars; beat until well blended. Add egg and beat well. Add vanilla and ½ cup orange-juice concentrate (reserve remainder for icing); mix to blend.

3. Gradually add flour mixture until just blended. Add coconut and pecans and stir until thoroughly combined.

4. Drop by level tablespoons about 2 inches apart onto greased baking sheets. Bake until cookies are golden brown and feel firm when touched lightly (12 to 14 minutes). Let stand for 1 to 2 minutes on baking sheets, then remove to wire racks.

5. While cookies are still warm, drizzle with Orange Icing.

Makes about 5 dozen 3-inch cookies.

Orange Icing In a small bowl, combine sugar and butter. Gradually blend in orange-juice concentrate until icing is smooth and of a good drizzling consistency.

GLAZED APPLE-SPICE DROPS

These spicy cookies are complemented by their cider-flavored icing.

- 1¾ cups flour
- 1 teaspoon each baking soda and ground cinnamon
- ½ teaspoon ground nutmeg
- ¼ teaspoon each salt and ground cloves
- ½ cup butter or margarine, softened
- 1½ cups firmly packed brown sugar
- 1 egg
- ¼ cup cider or apple juice
- 1 large apple, peeled, cored, and finely chopped
- 1 cup chopped walnuts

Cider Glaze

- 1 cup confectioners' sugar
- 1 tablespoon butter or margarine, softened
- ½ teaspoon vanilla extract
- 1½ to 2 tablespoons cider or apple juice

1. In a bowl stir together flour, baking soda, cinnamon, nutmeg, salt, and cloves to combine well; set aside.

2. Preheat oven to 400° F. In mixer bowl combine butter and brown sugar, and beat until well blended. Beat in egg until fluffy.

3. Add flour mixture alternately with cider, mixing until smooth after each addition. Stir in apple and walnuts.

4. Drop by tablespoons, placed about 2 inches apart, onto lightly greased baking sheets. Bake until cookies are golden brown (about 10 minutes). Remove to wire racks; while warm, spread lightly with Cider Glaze.

Makes about 4 dozen 3-inch cookies.

Cider Glaze In a small bowl combine confectioners' sugar and butter. Add vanilla, then cider, and blend until mixture has a good spreading consistency.

LEMON-NUTMEG CHEWS

Buttery-rich and tart with lemon, these sugar-sprinkled cookies suggest a moist shortbread.

    2 cups flour
    1 teaspoon baking powder
    ¼ teaspoon each salt and
       ground nutmeg
    ¾ cup butter or margarine,
       softened
    1 cup firmly packed
       brown sugar
    2 egg yolks
    1 tablespoon lemon juice
    2 teaspoons grated lemon rind

Sugar-and-Spice Topping

    1 tablespoon sugar
    ⅛ teaspoon ground nutmeg

1. In a bowl stir together flour, baking powder, salt, and nutmeg to combine thoroughly; set aside.

2. Preheat oven to 375° F. In mixer bowl combine butter and brown sugar; beat until well blended. Add egg yolks, one at a time, beating until fluffy after each addition. Add lemon juice and lemon rind; mix to blend.

3. Gradually add flour mixture until just blended.

4. Drop by rounded teaspoons about 2 inches apart onto ungreased baking sheets. Sprinkle lightly with Sugar-and-Spice Topping. Bake until cookies brown lightly (10 to 12 minutes). Remove to wire racks to cool.

Makes about 4 dozen 2-inch cookies.

Sugar-and-Spice Topping In a small bowl combine sugar and nutmeg; stir to blend.

There's spicy apple cider in these moist, cakelike Glazed Apple-Spice Drops. Cider is also in the glaze; spread it over the cookies while they are still warm from the oven.

17

OATMEAL COOKIES

Cookie fanciers know it is wise to keep rolled oats on the pantry shelf, even if mornings are too hurried to sit down to a steaming bowl of cooked oatmeal. In drop cookies, oatmeal replaces part of the flour, bringing a chewy texture and nutlike flavor that are an unforgettable part of enjoying these treats.

ORANGE-DATE OATMEAL ROUNDS

These plump oatmeal cookies have a classic look and some unexpected elements as well.

>   2 cups flour
>   1 teaspoon baking soda
>   ½ teaspoon salt
>   1 cup butter or margarine, softened
>   1 cup each granulated sugar and firmly packed brown sugar
>   2 eggs
>   1 tablespoon grated orange rind
>   3 tablespoons orange juice
>   3 cups quick-cooking rolled oats
>   1 cup finely chopped pitted dates
>   1 cup chopped walnuts

1. In a bowl stir together flour, baking soda, and salt to combine thoroughly; set aside.

2. Preheat oven to 350° F. In mixer bowl combine butter and sugars; beat until fluffy and well blended. Add eggs, one at a time, beating well after each addition. Beat in orange rind and orange juice.

3. Gradually add flour mixture until just blended. Stir in rolled oats, dates, and walnuts.

4. Drop by rounded tablespoons, placed about 2 inches apart, onto ungreased baking sheets. Bake until cookies feel firm in center when touched lightly and edges are brown (16 to 18 minutes). Transfer to wire racks to cool.

Makes about 4 dozen 3-inch cookies.

TRADITIONAL RAISIN-OATMEAL COOKIES

The first version of these pleasantly spicy cookies is crisp on the outside and chewy to the bite. The second version—made with simmered dried apricots—is more tart and moist.

>   1½ cups flour
>   1 teaspoon baking soda
>   ½ teaspoon ground cinnamon
>   ¼ teaspoon each salt, ground nutmeg, and ground cloves
>   ¾ cup butter or margarine, softened
>   1½ cups firmly packed brown sugar
>   2 eggs
>   1 teaspoon vanilla extract
>   2 cups quick-cooking rolled oats
>   1 cup raisins

1. In a bowl stir together flour, baking soda, cinnamon, salt, nutmeg, and cloves to combine thoroughly; set aside.

2. Preheat oven to 375° F. In mixer bowl combine butter and brown sugar, and beat until well blended. Add eggs, one at a time, beating well after each addition. Add vanilla and mix to blend.

3. Gradually add flour mixture until just blended. Stir in rolled oats and raisins.

4. Drop by tablespoons, placed about 2 inches apart, onto lightly greased baking sheets. Bake until cookies are lightly browned (about 10 minutes). Cool on wire racks.

Makes about 4 dozen 2½-inch cookies.

Apricot-Oatmeal Drops Omit raisins. Using kitchen scissors, cut 1 cup dried apricots into thin slivers. Place in a medium saucepan with 1 cup water. Bring to a boil over high heat; reduce heat and simmer, uncovered, until apricots can be pierced easily with a fork (8 to 10 minutes). Drain well and pat dry with paper towels. Add apricots to cookie dough along with rolled oats and ½ cup chopped walnuts.

Makes about 5 dozen cookies.

RANGER COOKIES

All kinds of community cookbooks have included this recipe in one form or another. It can probably be traced to the test kitchen of one of the giant cereal companies. Although more than 50 years old, the recipe is still frequently requested. If you have never tasted this appealing combination of oatmeal, crisp rice cereal, and coconut, you are in store for a delicious surprise.

>   1 cup flour
>   ½ teaspoon baking soda
>   ¼ teaspoon baking powder
>   ⅛ teaspoon salt
>   ½ cup butter or margarine, softened
>   ½ cup each granulated sugar and firmly packed brown sugar
>   1 egg
>   1 teaspoon vanilla extract
>   1 cup each quick-cooking rolled oats and ready-to-eat crisp rice cereal
>   ½ cup flaked coconut

1. In a bowl stir together flour, baking soda, baking powder, and salt to combine thoroughly; set aside.

2. Preheat oven to 375° F. In mixer bowl combine butter and sugars. Beat until fluffy and well blended; beat in egg. Add vanilla and mix well.

3. Gradually add flour mixture until just blended. Stir in rolled oats, rice cereal, and coconut.

4. Drop by rounded teaspoons, placed slightly apart, onto lightly greased or nonstick baking sheets. Bake until cookies are golden brown (about 10 minutes). Remove at once to wire racks to cool.

Makes about forty-two 2½-inch cookies.

These tempting cookies include (left to right) Apricot-Oatmeal Drops, Double Chocolate-Chip Oatmeal Cookies (page 20), and Ranger Cookies.

DOUBLE CHOCOLATE-CHIP OATMEAL COOKIES

Who ever said that oatmeal cookies had to be sensible? This crisp, rich interpretation is made with both cocoa and a generous measure of chocolate chips. The recipe makes nearly 100 cookies, so you can freeze some of them (see page 48).

  1¼ cups flour
  ⅓ cup unsweetened cocoa
  ½ teaspoon each baking soda and salt
  1 cup butter or margarine, softened
  1 cup granulated sugar
  ½ cup firmly packed brown sugar
  1 egg
  1 teaspoon vanilla extract
  ¼ cup water
  3 cups quick-cooking rolled oats
  1 package (12 oz) semisweet chocolate chips

1. In a bowl stir together flour, cocoa, baking soda, and salt to combine thoroughly; set aside.

2. Preheat oven to 350° F. In mixer bowl combine butter and sugars; beat until fluffy and well blended. Beat in egg. Add vanilla and mix well.

3. Add flour mixture alternately with the water, mixing until smooth after each addition. Stir in rolled oats, then chocolate chips.

4. Drop by rounded teaspoons, placed about 1½ inches apart, onto ungreased baking sheets. Bake until almost no indentation remains when tops of cookies are touched lightly (10 to 12 minutes). Let stand on baking sheets for 1 to 2 minutes, then remove to wire racks to finish cooling.

Makes about 8 dozen 2½-inch cookies.

ABUNDANTLY NUTTY COOKIES

Nuts of all sorts are a favorite ingredient in many kinds of cookies. Buy them in bulk when you see them at a good price. The following recipes have been singled out to show off nuts to the most tantalizing advantage.

CHOCOLATE-WALNUT BUTTONS

A little hollow pressed into each of these walnut-speckled cookies will hold a cache of fudgy frosting after the cookies bake.

  1⅔ cups flour
  ½ teaspoon each salt and baking soda
  ½ cup butter or margarine, softened
  ½ cup firmly packed brown sugar
  ¼ cup granulated sugar
  1 egg
  ½ teaspoon vanilla extract
  1 cup chopped walnuts

Chocolate Frosting

  ¼ cup butter or margarine
  1 square (1 oz) unsweetened chocolate
  2 tablespoons milk
  1½ cups confectioners' sugar
  ½ teaspoon vanilla extract

1. In a bowl stir together flour, salt, and baking soda to combine thoroughly; set aside.

2. Preheat oven to 375° F. In mixer bowl combine butter and brown and granulated sugars; beat until fluffy and well blended. Beat in egg until fluffy. Add vanilla and mix well.

3. Gradually add flour mixture until just blended. Stir in walnuts.

4. Drop by rounded teaspoons slightly apart onto ungreased baking sheets. With your finger or teaspoon, make a depression in center of each cookie. Bake cookies for 5 minutes. Press depressions down again, then continue baking until cookies are golden brown (4 to 5 minutes).

5. Transfer cookies to wire racks to cool. Fill centers with frosting, dividing it evenly.

Makes about 4 dozen 2-inch cookies.

Chocolate Frosting In top of a double boiler over simmering water, combine butter and chocolate. Heat, stirring occasionally, until chocolate melts. Blend in milk. Remove from heat; mix in confectioners' sugar and vanilla until smooth.

CRISP DUTCH ALMOND COOKIES

Rolling dollops of drop-cookie dough in sliced almonds coats each one—top and bottom—with nuts.

  1⅓ cups flour
  ½ teaspoon baking powder
  ¾ cup butter or margarine, softened
  ½ cup each granulated sugar and firmly packed brown sugar
  ½ teaspoon each vanilla and almond extract
  2 tablespoons water
  1 cup (approximately) sliced almonds

1. In a bowl stir together flour and baking powder to combine thoroughly; set aside.

2. Preheat oven to 325° F. In mixer bowl combine butter and sugars; beat until fluffy and well blended. Mix in vanilla and almond extract.

3. Add flour mixture to butter mixture alternately with the water, blending until smooth after each addition.

4. Spread almonds in a shallow pan. Drop dough by heaping teaspoons into almonds. Roll each cookie to coat well, adding almonds as needed.

5. Place cookies about 1 inch apart on ungreased baking sheets. Bake until lightly browned (15 to 20 minutes). Let stand on baking sheets for about 1 minute, then transfer to wire racks to complete cooling.

Makes about 3 dozen 2½-inch cookies.

MACADAMIA CRISPS

Elegant macadamia nuts are the perfect choice for these thin, crisp, butter-rich cookies. Serve them with sweet cherries for a simple but sublime dessert of finger foods.

> 1 cup flour
> ¼ teaspoon baking soda
> ½ cup butter or margarine, softened
> 1¼ cups firmly packed brown sugar
> 1 egg
> 1 teaspoon vanilla extract
> 1 cup chopped macadamia nuts

1. In a bowl stir together flour and baking soda to combine thoroughly; set aside.

2. Preheat oven to 375° F. In mixer bowl combine butter and brown sugar, and beat until well blended. Beat in egg until fluffy. Add vanilla and mix to blend.

3. Gradually add flour mixture until just blended. Stir in macadamia nuts.

4. Drop by rounded teaspoons, placed about 1½ inches apart, onto lightly greased baking sheets. Bake until cookies are golden brown (8 to 10 minutes). Let stand briefly on baking sheets, then remove to wire racks to cool completely.

Makes about 5 dozen 2½-inch cookies.

Mending seems less tedious when sweetened by a crunchy chocolate-nut treat such as Chocolate-Walnut Buttons, along with a cup of your favorite tea.

Icing-drizzled Frosted Pecan Drops will remind you of that New Orleans favorite, pecan pralines, baked into crisp cookies.

SPICY DATE-WALNUT DROPS

Whole wheat flour used in these fragrantly spiced cookies enhances their nutlike flavor.

1½ cups whole wheat flour
1 teaspoon baking powder
2 teaspoons ground allspice
½ teaspoon baking soda
¼ teaspoon salt
1 cup butter or margarine, softened
1 cup firmly packed brown sugar
2 eggs
¼ cup sherry or apple juice
½ cup chopped pitted dates
1 cup chopped walnuts

Sugar Glaze

1½ cups confectioners' sugar
2 teaspoons butter or margarine, softened
½ teaspoon vanilla extract
2 to 3 tablespoons warm water

1. In a medium bowl stir together flour, baking powder, allspice, baking soda, and salt to combine thoroughly; set aside.

2. Preheat oven to 350° F. In mixer bowl combine butter and brown sugar; beat until fluffy and well blended. Add eggs, one at a time, beating well after each addition.

3. Add flour mixture alternately with sherry, mixing until smooth after each addition. Stir in dates and walnuts.

4. Drop by tablespoons, placed about 1½ inches apart, onto ungreased baking sheets. Bake until edges of cookies are brown and tops feel firm when touched lightly (10 to 12 minutes).

5. Remove to wire racks. While cookies are warm, spread a little Sugar Glaze over each one. Cool completely before serving or storing.

Makes about 4 dozen 3-inch cookies.

Sugar Glaze In a small bowl combine confectioners' sugar, butter, and vanilla. Gradually blend in the water until icing is smooth and of a good consistency for spreading.

SPICED PEANUT COOKIES

Salted cocktail peanuts are the surprise ingredient in these spicy oatmeal cookies. The cookies stay crisp and fresh in a covered container for several days.

1 cup flour
½ teaspoon each baking powder, baking soda, and ground cinnamon
¼ teaspoon ground nutmeg
½ cup butter or margarine, softened
1 cup firmly packed brown sugar
1 egg
½ teaspoon vanilla extract
1 cup each quick-cooking rolled oats and salted Spanish peanuts

1. In a bowl stir together flour, baking powder, baking soda, cinnamon, and nutmeg to combine thoroughly; set aside.

2. Preheat oven to 375° F. In mixer bowl combine butter and brown sugar. Beat until well blended, then beat in egg until fluffy. Add vanilla and mix to blend.

3. Gradually add flour mixture until just blended. Stir in rolled oats and peanuts.

4. Drop by rounded teaspoons, placed slightly apart, onto lightly greased baking sheets. Bake until cookies are golden brown (about 8 minutes). Cool on wire racks.

Makes about 5 dozen 2-inch cookies.

FROSTED PECAN DROPS

A cookie version of pralines, these icing-drizzled wafers are both chewy and crisp.

1½ cups flour
1½ teaspoons baking powder
¼ teaspoon salt
½ cup butter or margarine, softened
1½ cups firmly packed brown sugar
1 egg
1 teaspoon vanilla extract
1 cup pecans, coarsely chopped

Praline Icing

1 cup firmly packed brown sugar
½ cup whipping cream
1 cup confectioners' sugar

1. In a bowl stir together flour, baking powder, and salt to combine thoroughly; set aside.

2. Preheat oven to 350° F. In mixer bowl combine butter and brown sugar. Beat until well blended, then beat in egg until fluffy. Add vanilla and mix to blend.

3. Gradually add flour mixture until just blended.

4. Drop by rounded teaspoons, placed slightly apart, onto lightly greased baking sheets. Flatten each cookie slightly with a fork. Sprinkle with pecans, using about ¾ teaspoon of nuts for each cookie. Bake until golden brown (about 10 minutes). Transfer at once to wire racks.

5. Drizzle cooled cookies generously with icing.

Makes about 4 dozen 2½-inch cookies.

Praline Icing

1. In a 1½- to 2-quart saucepan, combine brown sugar and whipping cream. Place over medium-high heat, stirring until sugar dissolves and cream comes to a boil. Boil, stirring constantly, for 1 minute.

2. Remove from heat and blend in confectioners' sugar. Beat until smooth, then use at once.

Lemon Cookie Stacks, an elegant dessert, intersperse crisp Lemon Roof-Tile Cookies with an ethereal, raspberry-studded lemon-mousse filling.

TILE AND LACE COOKIES

A drop-cookie batter, baked wafer thin, produces cookies of remarkable flexibility. While still warm from the oven, they can be rolled or curled into a variety of whimsical shapes.

As delightful as these delicate cookies are in their unadorned state, they can also serve as the ethereal structure for an irresistible dessert.

LEMON ROOF-TILE COOKIES

Curved into distinctive U shapes or twirled into "cigarettes" or cones, French *tuiles au citron* are a classic accompaniment to homemade ice cream or sorbet. They can also be baked as large cookies, then shaped into stylized tulips as edible containers for a frozen dessert. Although crisp when they are freshly baked, they may absorb moisture from the air and soften after standing. You can restore their crispness by arranging the cookies in a single layer on a baking sheet and placing them in a 200° F oven for 20 to 30 minutes.

> ¼ cup blanched almonds
> ⅓ cup sifted cake flour
> ¼ cup butter or margarine, softened
> ½ cup sugar
> 2 egg whites (about ¼ cup)
> ¼ teaspoon lemon extract
> 1 tablespoon grated lemon rind
> ½ cup (approximately) sliced almonds (optional)

1. In blender or food processor whirl blanched almonds until powdery. In a small bowl combine almonds with cake flour, stirring to blend thoroughly. Set aside.

2. Preheat oven to 400° F. Grease baking sheets and dust with flour (or line baking sheets with lightly buttered parchment paper).

3. In mixer bowl combine butter and sugar; beat until light and fluffy. Beat in egg whites until well blended. Stir in lemon extract and lemon rind. Gradually add flour mixture, beating until smooth.

4. Drop batter onto prepared baking sheets by rounded teaspoons, about 2 inches apart, to make tiles as shown in step 1, or cones or cigarettes as shown in step 2. Batter can also be dropped by level tablespoons, about 3 inches apart, to make tulips as shown in step 3. Sprinkle each with sliced almonds, if desired, to cover sparsely. With small spatula or back of a spoon, spread batter to a 3-inch-diameter circle for tiles or cones or to a 4-inch-diameter circle for tulips.

5. Bake until edges of cookies are brown (4 to 6 minutes). Let stand on baking sheets until cookies are barely firm enough to handle but still pliable (30 seconds to 1 minute). Carefully remove with a spatula and shape into tiles, cones, cigarettes, or tulips as shown at right, or transfer to wire racks to make flat cookies.

6. If cookies become too cool to shape, return to oven for a few seconds until they are pliable again.

Makes about 30 small or 16 large cookies.

LEMON COOKIE STACKS

Inspired by a dessert served at the stylish Paris restaurant Apicius, this recipe layers flat Lemon Roof-Tile Cookies, fresh lemon mousse, and raspberries, then surrounds them with lemon and apricot sauce.

    16 Lemon Roof-Tile Cookies,
        baked as 4½- to 5-inch flat
        cookies
    ¼   cup butter or margarine
    2   teaspoons grated lemon rind
    ¼   cup lemon juice
    ⅔   cup sugar
    2   eggs
    3   tablespoons apricot nectar
    ½   cup whipping cream
    1   pint raspberries
        Vanilla Confectioners' Sugar
        (see page 39)
        Mint sprigs, for garnish

1. Prepare flat Lemon Roof-Tile Cookies, using a rounded tablespoon of batter for each. Let flat cookies cool on wire racks, then set aside for up to 8 hours.

2. To make base for filling and sauce, in top of a double boiler melt butter over direct low heat. Remove from heat and add lemon rind, lemon juice, sugar, and eggs; beat with a whisk until well combined.

3. Place lemon mixture over simmering water; cook, stirring often, until mixture is thickened and smooth (about 10 minutes). Remove top of double boiler to a wire rack and let stand until lemon filling is barely warm to the touch.

4. Transfer ⅓ cup of the lemon filling to a small bowl. Gradually blend in apricot nectar until sauce is smooth; set aside.

5. In a medium bowl whip cream until stiff; fold in remaining lemon filling, then 1 cup of the raspberries.

6. Place 1 cookie on each of 4 plates. Spread with a little whipped cream filling. Cover each with a second and third cookie, lightly spreading each with whipped cream filling. Lightly sift Vanilla Confectioners' Sugar over 4 remaining cookies; place 1 atop each serving.

7. Spoon a fourth of the apricot-lemon sauce around each serving. Garnish with remaining raspberries and mint sprigs; serve immediately.

Makes 4 servings.

PECAN LACE COOKIES

These cookies can be shaped and served in all the ways suggested for Lemon Roof-Tile Cookies. Shaped into tulips, they are delectable filled with apple or butter-pecan ice cream and topped with hot caramel sauce.

    ¼   cup butter or margarine
    ¼   cup firmly packed brown
        sugar
    ¼   cup light corn syrup
    ⅓   cup flour
    ½   cup finely chopped pecans
    1   teaspoon vanilla extract

1. Preheat oven to 350° F. Grease baking sheets and dust with flour.

2. Melt butter in a 1½- to 2-quart saucepan over medium heat. Stir in brown sugar and corn syrup. Increase heat to high and bring mixture to a boil, stirring constantly until brown sugar dissolves.

3. Remove pan from heat. Stir in flour and pecans until well combined. Blend in vanilla.

4. Drop batter onto prepared baking sheets by rounded teaspoons, placed about 2 inches apart, to make tiles as shown in step 1 or cigarettes or cones as shown in step 2, or drop by rounded tablespoons, placed about 3 inches apart, to make tulips as shown in step 3. With small spatula spread batter into an even circle.

5. Bake until cookies are browned (6 to 8 minutes for small cookies, 8 to 10 minutes for large ones). Let stand on baking sheets until cookies are barely firm enough to handle (30 seconds to 1 minute). Remove carefully with a spatula and shape as shown at right, or transfer to wire racks to make flat cookies.

6. If cookies become too cool to shape, return to oven briefly.

Makes about 30 small or 8 to 10 large cookies.

TILE AND LACE COOKIES

1. *Remove warm tile or lace cookies, one at a time, from baking sheet and immediately drape over rolling pin (for small cookies, use small rolling pin) or curl in metal baguette pan. After cookies are cool transfer to wire rack. If you use sliced almonds in dough, drape or roll cookies so nutty sides are up.*

2. *Roll each warm cookie around buttered handle of wooden spoon or cone. Remove when cool.*

3. *Let each lace cookie cool on baking sheet until just firm enough to handle. Drape, bumpy side down, over inverted 2½- to 3-inch-diameter drinking glass, pressing draped portions of cookie softly into a cup shape. When cookies are set, transfer to wire rack or carefully place on baking sheet.*

Traditional Italian cookies—hazelnut meringues (page 28) and almond macaroons (page 29)—appear in a contemporary setting.

COOKIE-BAKING HINTS

When you bake drop cookies, following these simple procedures will make every step easier.

Use vegetable shortening or a non-stick vegetable spray (not butter) when a recipe specifies greased baking sheets. (There's no need to grease baking sheets unless a recipe says you should.)

To shape drop cookies, use two spoons. Scoop up the specified amount of dough with one, then use the other to help transfer the dough onto the baking sheet. Use both spoons to shape the spoonful of dough into a smoothly rounded mound. Try to make all the cookies uniform in size and shape so they will finish baking at the same time.

Good circulation of hot air in the oven is needed to bake cookies evenly. In general, use the middle oven rack, positioning a single baking sheet in the center of it. If you have a wide oven, you may be able to place two narrow baking sheets side by side, but you should allow at least 1 inch of space between them, and between the baking sheets and sides of the oven.

If time dictates baking two sheets of cookies at once, place one baking sheet on one side of the upper oven rack and the other baking sheet on the other side of the center rack. Halfway through the baking time, reverse the position of the two sheets.

Some cookies are sturdy enough to be removed to cooling racks as soon as they come from the oven. Others are more delicate and must first cool slightly on the baking sheet. Each recipe tells you how the cookies should be cooled, but be aware that fragile cookies should be treated with a light hand.

Let baking sheets cool between uses. If you drop cookie dough onto a hot baking sheet, it will begin to spread or even bake before all the cookies are in place.

ALMOST FLOURLESS COOKIES

Although flour is the backbone of most cookies, some can be made without it. Such cookies take their substance from well-beaten whole eggs or egg whites, finely chopped or ground nuts, or even fine bread crumbs. Although almost flourless cookies aren't short on flavor, they tend to seem lighter, and most use a minimum of butter or shortening.

PECAN-CRUMB MACAROONS

Made with fine, dry bread crumbs, these light cookies are delicately crisp and seem almost like lace.

>   1 cup each *fine, dry bread crumbs and finely chopped pecans*
>   1 cup sugar
>   ⅛ teaspoon salt
>   2 eggs, at room temperature
>   1 teaspoon vanilla extract

1. In a large bowl combine bread crumbs, pecans, ¾ cup of the sugar, and salt. Stir to combine thoroughly.

2. Preheat oven to 350° F. In mixer bowl beat eggs until thick and light colored. Beat in vanilla, then gradually beat in remaining ¼ cup sugar.

3. Add beaten eggs to crumb mixture. Lightly fold together to blend well.

4. Drop by rounded teaspoons, placed about 1½ inches apart, onto well-greased baking sheets. Bake until cookies feel firm when touched gently and are lightly browned (12 to 15 minutes). Carefully remove at once to cooling racks.

Makes about 4 dozen 2½-inch cookies.

ITALIAN HAZELNUT MERINGUES

These crisp meringue cookies studded with toasted hazelnuts and candied orange peel are fragrant with nutmeg and Marsala. They are excellent as a light accompaniment to an after-dinner wine such as port. The recipe directs you to remove the skins from the hazelnuts before chopping. This isn't strictly necessary, but do be sure to toast the nuts for the time given, for added flavor.

>   1 cup unblanched hazelnuts
>   3 egg whites (6 tablespoons)
>   ¼ teaspoon cream of tartar
>   ⅛ teaspoon ground nutmeg
>   1 cup sugar
>   1 tablespoon Marsala or 1 teaspoon vanilla extract
>   2 tablespoons finely chopped candied orange peel

1. Preheat oven to 350° F. Spread hazelnuts in a shallow pan. Bake until lightly browned (8 to 10 minutes). After removing nuts from oven, reduce temperature to 300° F. Let nuts cool slightly, then rub off and discard most of the brown skins. Chop nuts finely and set aside.

2. Line baking sheets with baking parchment or brown wrapping paper.

3. In mixer bowl combine egg whites, cream of tartar, and nutmeg. Beat at high speed until foamy. Gradually add sugar, beating until mixture is stiff and glossy.

4. Beat in Marsala. Blend in hazelnuts and orange peel.

5. Drop by rounded teaspoons, placed about 2 inches apart, onto paper-lined baking sheets. Bake until cookies feel firm when touched lightly (25 to 30 minutes). Remove to wire racks to cool.

Makes about fifty-four 2-inch cookies.

CLAIRE'S WALNUT COOKIES

Light yet rich, these chewy cookies capture the sweet and toasty quality of the walnuts that make up most of their substance.

> 1 cup firmly packed
> brown sugar
> 2 tablespoons flour, plus
> flour for dusting
> ¼ teaspoon ground cinnamon
> 1 egg white (2 tablespoons)
> ⅛ teaspoon cream of tartar
> 1 teaspoon vanilla extract
> 1¼ cups finely chopped walnuts

1. Grease baking sheets and dust with flour, shaking off excess. Preheat oven to 325° F.

2. In a large bowl stir together brown sugar, flour, and cinnamon to combine thoroughly; set aside.

3. Combine egg white and cream of tartar in mixer bowl. Beat at high speed until moist, stiff peaks form. Fold into sugar mixture to moisten it. Add vanilla and walnuts; mix lightly to combine well.

4. Drop by rounded teaspoons, placed about 2 inches apart, onto prepared baking sheets. Bake until cookies feel firm when touched gently and are lightly browned (about 15 minutes). Let stand on baking sheets for about 5 minutes, then remove carefully to wire racks to complete cooling.

Makes about thirty 2-inch cookies.

SIENESE ALMOND MACAROONS

The Tuscan city of Siena claims credit for these distinctive, ground-almond ovals, known there as *ricciarelli*.

> 1⅓ cups blanched almonds
> 1 teaspoon almond extract
> ¼ cup granulated sugar
> 2 tablespoons flour
> 1¼ cups confectioners' sugar
> 2 egg whites (¼ cup), slightly beaten

1. Freeze almonds so they can be ground easily. Place frozen almonds in food processor or blender (if using blender, work with only about half of the frozen almonds at a time). Process or whirl until almonds have the consistency of coarse meal. Set aside.

2. Line baking sheets with baking parchment or brown wrapping paper; grease paper lightly. Preheat oven to 325° F.

3. In a large bowl combine ground almonds and almond extract. Add granulated sugar, flour, and ¾ cup of the confectioners' sugar; stir to combine thoroughly. Blend in egg whites until mixture holds together.

4. Drop by scant tablespoons, placed about 2 inches apart, onto paper-lined baking sheets. Using a spoon and a small spatula, shape each drop into an oval. Sift ¼ cup of the remaining confectioners' sugar evenly over the cookies.

5. Bake until cookies feel firm and dry to the touch and are barely browned (16 to 18 minutes). Sift remaining ¼ cup confectioners' sugar evenly over warm cookies. Let stand on baking sheets for about 5 minutes before transferring to wire racks to cool completely.

Makes about 2 dozen cookies.

Tips

PREPARING NUTS

Nuts add a delicious texture to all kinds of cookies. Prepare and measure them before you begin making the cookie dough.

Ground or very finely chopped nuts can be prepared in a blender or food processor. When using a blender, turn the motor on and off several times until the nuts reach the desired consistency, alternately scraping down the sides of the container with a spatula.

Large amounts of nuts can be ground or finely chopped more successfully in a food processor. Freezing the nuts first makes them easier to process uniformly. (Storing nuts in the freezer is also a good idea in warm weather; it prevents the oil in the nuts from becoming rancid.)

A small, hand-operated nut grinder can also be used to chop nuts finely. Be sure it has a cutting blade that is sturdy enough to handle hard nuts such as almonds and hazelnuts.

Nuts can also be chopped neatly with a French chef's knife that has a sharp, long blade. Spread nuts in a single layer on a heavy cutting board and use the same pivoting action you would employ to chop onions or parsley. A long-bladed knife is really the easiest and most efficient tool for chopping nuts coarsely—when you want chunky nuts in chocolate-chip cookies or brownies, for example.

Toasting nuts to bring out their flavor is suggested in some recipes. Preheat the oven to 350° F. Spread the nuts in a single layer in a shallow baking pan. Bake nuts until they are golden brown (usually between 8 and 10 minutes). Smaller nuts, such as pine nuts or slivered almonds, may toast more rapidly; check them after about 6 minutes.

White-Chocolate Brownies (see page 36) are an irresistible invitation to the delicious world of bar cookies.

Bar Cookies

Cookies baked in a straight-sided pan and then cut into bars are convenient when time is short. The batter is quickly prepared and put into the oven at once; you can attend to other matters while the cookies bake. Such cookies can take several forms—classic fudge brownies; crisp, buttery shortbread; bars made in two or more varied and delicious layers; and long, somewhat free-form strips. They are all cut apart after baking.

ALL KINDS OF BROWNIES

Brownies are the ultimate bar cookies. In their purest form, chocolate flavor permeates every crumb; and coarsely chopped nuts are strewn throughout for crunchy contrast to the overall moistness.

Close your eyes and the great pleasures associated with brownies come to mind—a slumber party where no one cared about calories; an unforgettable picnic; the otherwise undistinguished dinner where brownies fresh from the oven, topped with ice cream, saved your reputation as a hostess.

There are nearly as many ways to bake a brownie as there are delicious recollections associated with them.

CLASSIC FUDGE BROWNIES

There is very little flour—but lots of chocolate—in these brownies, so they are moist textured and intensely flavored. For a taste of mocha, try the Espresso Brownies variation.

- *3 squares (3 oz) unsweetened chocolate*
- *½ cup butter or margarine*
- *⅓ cup flour*
- *½ teaspoon baking powder*
- *¼ teaspoon salt*
- *2 eggs, at room temperature*
- *½ cup each granulated sugar and firmly packed brown sugar*
- *1 teaspoon vanilla extract*
- *1 cup coarsely chopped walnuts*

1. Preheat oven to 350° F. Combine chocolate and butter in a small, heavy saucepan over low heat. Let stand until melted, then stir well to blend. Let chocolate mixture cool while continuing with step 2.

2. Grease an 8-inch-square pan; dust with flour. In a small bowl stir together flour, baking powder, and salt to combine thoroughly; set aside.

3. In mixer bowl combine eggs and sugars; beat at high speed until thick. Blend in vanilla, then chocolate mixture. Gradually add flour mixture, beating until well combined. Stir in walnuts.

4. Spread batter in prepared pan. Bake until edges pull away from sides of pan and center is nearly set when tested with a toothpick (24 to 28 minutes). Do not overbake.

5. Let cool in pan on a wire rack for about 10 minutes, then cut into bars. Remove from pan when cool.

Makes 18 bars.

Espresso Brownies Add 1 teaspoon powdered or granulated instant coffee to chocolate-butter mixture as it melts.

BUTTERSCOTCH SAUCEPAN BROWNIES

The pecan-studded batter for these buttery blond brownies is mixed in one saucepan to simplify the preparation.

- *1 cup flour*
- *¾ teaspoon baking powder*
- *Pinch salt*
- *⅓ cup butter or margarine*
- *1 cup firmly packed brown sugar*
- *1 egg*
- *1 teaspoon vanilla extract*
- *½ cup chopped pecans*

1. In a bowl stir together flour, baking powder, and salt to combine thoroughly; set aside.

2. Preheat oven to 350° F. Grease an 8-inch-square pan; dust with flour.

3. Place butter in a 2-quart saucepan over medium heat until melted. Add brown sugar, stirring until sugar dissolves and mixture bubbles. Remove from heat and let stand for 5 minutes to cool slightly.

4. Beat in egg and vanilla, then gradually stir in flour mixture. Add pecans and mix well. Spread batter in prepared pan.

5. Bake until edges begin to pull away from sides of pan and a toothpick inserted in center comes out with just a few crumbs (25 to 30 minutes).

6. Let stand in pan on a wire rack for about 10 minutes, then cut into bars. Remove from pan when cool.

Makes 18 bars.

SWEDISH ALMOND BROWNIES

Almonds and a hint of bitter-almond flavor are the Scandinavian touches in these delicately thin brownies.

- *1½ squares (1½ oz) unsweetened chocolate*
- *½ cup butter or margarine*
- *2 eggs, at room temperature*
- *1 cup granulated sugar*
- *¼ teaspoon almond extract*
- *⅓ cup flour*
- *½ cup sliced almonds*
- *Confectioners' sugar*

1. Preheat oven to 400° F. Combine chocolate and butter in a small, heavy saucepan over low heat. Let stand until melted, then stir well to blend. Let chocolate mixture cool while continuing with step 2.

2. Grease a 9- by 13-inch pan; dust with flour. In mixer bowl beat eggs at high speed until thick and light colored. Gradually add granulated sugar, beating until well combined.

3. Stir in chocolate mixture and almond extract until blended. Mix in flour, then almonds.

4. Spread batter in prepared pan. Bake until top springs back when touched lightly (15 to 18 minutes).

5. Let cool in pan on a wire rack for about 5 minutes, then cut into bars. Sift lightly with confectioners' sugar. Remove from pan when cool.

Makes 30 bars.

Choose your favorite (left to right): Classic Fudge Brownies, Marbled Cream-Cheese Brownies (page 36), or Chocolate–Brown-Sugar Brownies (page 37).

LAYERED BROWNIE TORTE

Dark and dense with chocolate, a moist, homemade brownie is a chocolate lover's dream come true. There are those, however, who feel that if chocolate is good, more chocolate is even better. It's hard for those with such a sensibility to resist the impulse to embellish the classic brownie. Here is a triple-chocolate brownie dessert reminiscent of the renowned *Sachertorte*. Serve this confection with clouds of whipped cream or, as it's said along the Danube, *mit Schlag*.

BROWNIE FANTASY TORTE

This splendid party dessert lends itself to some advance preparation. If you wish, prepare the Cocoa Pastry through step 1 as much as a day ahead. If you prepare it earlier than that, plan to freeze the pastry in the pan at this stage. Be sure to place the pan on a flat surface in the freezer to avoid dislodging the removable bottom and breaking the pastry.

The brownie filling will be at its peak of moistness if baked the same day as it is served. To preserve the glossy sheen of the chocolate decoration, apply it no more than four hours before serving.

You may vary the flavor of the classic *Sachertorte* combination of apricot and chocolate by substituting raspberry preserves or sophisticated ginger marmalade for the apricot jam, which is nestled between the chocolate pastry and the brownie filling. Finely chopped hazelnuts or pecans can replace the sliced almonds for another change of flavor.

½ cup apricot jam or preserves
3 squares (3 oz) unsweetened chocolate
½ cup butter or margarine
⅓ cup flour
¼ teaspoon baking powder
⅛ teaspoon salt
2 eggs, at room temperature
1 cup sugar
1 teaspoon vanilla extract
⅓ cup sliced almonds
1 square (1 oz) semisweet baking chocolate
½ teaspoon salad oil
Whipped cream (optional)

Cocoa Pastry

1¼ cups flour
2 tablespoons unsweetened cocoa
⅓ cup Vanilla Confectioners' Sugar (see page 39)
½ cup firm butter or margarine
1 egg yolk
1 tablespoon water

1. Preheat oven to 350° F. Press Cocoa Pastry evenly and firmly over bottom and up sides of a 10½- to 11-inch removable-bottom tart pan. Bake for 12 minutes. Remove from oven and cool in pan on a wire rack.

2. When pastry is cool to the touch, spread apricot jam evenly over bottom of pastry shell. Set aside while preparing brownie filling.

3. In a small, heavy pan over low heat, combine unsweetened chocolate and butter. Let stand until melted, then stir to blend. Let cool while continuing with step 4.

4. In a small bowl stir together flour, baking powder, and salt to combine thoroughly; set aside.

5. In mixer bowl combine eggs and sugar; beat at high speed until thick. Blend in vanilla, then chocolate mixture. Gradually add flour mixture, beating until well combined. Stir in almonds.

6. Spread batter in jam-lined pastry. Return to 350° F oven and bake until center is nearly set when tested with a toothpick (20 to 25 minutes).

7. Remove from oven and let torte cool in pan on a wire rack. Then carefully remove sides of pan and transfer torte to a serving plate.

8. In a small, heavy pan over low heat, melt semisweet baking chocolate with oil. Using a paper cone (see page 109) or the tip of a teaspoon, drizzle melted chocolate over surface of torte. Set aside until chocolate is firm.

9. To serve, cut torte into wedges. Accompany with whipped cream (if desired).

Makes 8 to 10 servings.

Cocoa Pastry *To prepare by hand:* In a bowl stir together flour, cocoa, and Vanilla Confectioners' Sugar to combine thoroughly. Using a pastry blender or 2 knives, cut in butter until mixture resembles coarse crumbs. In a small bowl combine egg yolk and the water; beat until blended. Add egg mixture to flour mixture, stirring with a fork until dough clings together. Use your hands to press dough into a smooth ball. *To prepare in food processor:* Combine dry ingredients in work bowl and whirl to blend. Dice butter and add to work bowl; process using short on-off bursts. Then add egg mixture through feed tube, processing just until dough forms a ball.

BAKING BETTER BROWNIES—AND OTHER BARS

Each person's ideal brownie may be a bit different. But one characteristic most can agree on is that brownies should be slightly underbaked in the center. The proportions of chocolate, butter, eggs, and sugar in a recipe largely determine the degree of moist richness of the baked brownies. Another important factor is the baking time, which will vary depending on your oven as well as the surface and size of the baking pan. Remember that a cakelike brownie is usually an overbaked brownie.

☐ Brownies bake from the sides of the pan toward the center. Start testing for doneness when the edges begin to pull away from the sides of the pan.

☐ Touch the surface of the brownies lightly with your fingertip. If it seems set, use a cake tester for the final test.

☐ Insert a cake tester, slim bamboo skewer, or toothpick in the center. When it emerges with a few moist, clinging crumbs, it's time to remove the brownies from the oven.

☐ In general, let brownies and other bar cookies stand in the pan on a cooling rack until barely warm (usually 5 to 10 minutes) before cutting them into bars or squares. After you've cut the specified number of cookies, let them cool completely in the pan before removing them.

☐ Most bar cookies freeze well (see page 48). The richer and more buttery they are, the better they will take to freezing.

MARBLED CREAM-CHEESE BROWNIES

Two batters—one made with cream cheese, the other with melted semisweet chocolate and chopped nuts—are swirled together to make these unusual brownies. The light batter is similar to a cheesecake filling; the chocolate one is a classic brownie mixture. Combined, they form bars that are moist and flavorful.

Cream-Cheese Mixture

- 2 *tablespoons butter or margarine, softened*
- 1 *small package (3 oz) cream cheese, softened*
- ¼ *cup sugar*
- 1 *egg*
- 1 *tablespoon flour*
- ½ *teaspoon vanilla extract*

Chocolate Mixture

- 4 *ounces semisweet chocolate*
- 3 *tablespoons butter or margarine*
- ½ *cup flour*
- ½ *teaspoon baking powder*
- ¼ *teaspoon salt*
- 2 *eggs*
- ¾ *cup sugar*
- 1 *teaspoon vanilla extract*
- ½ *cup chopped walnuts*

1. *To prepare Cream-Cheese Mixture:* In mixer bowl combine butter and cream cheese; beat until well mixed. Add sugar and beat well. Add egg and beat until fluffy. Blend in flour and vanilla; set mixture aside.

2. *To prepare Chocolate Mixture:* Combine chocolate and butter in a small, heavy pan over low heat. Let stand until melted, then stir well to blend together. Let Chocolate Mixture cool while continuing with step 3.

3. Preheat oven to 350° F. Grease an 8-inch-square pan; dust with flour. In a bowl stir together flour, baking powder, and salt to combine thoroughly; set aside. In clean mixer bowl, using clean beaters, beat eggs at high speed until light colored. Gradually beat in sugar, then beat in vanilla. Gradually add flour mixture, mixing until well combined. Blend in Chocolate Mixture. Stir in walnuts.

4. Spread half of Chocolate Mixture in prepared pan. Pour Cream-Cheese Mixture over it, lightly spreading to pan edges. Cover with remaining Chocolate Mixture. Swirl a thin spatula through all three layers to create a marbled effect.

5. Bake until edges pull away from sides of pan and center is nearly set when tested with a toothpick (40 to 45 minutes).

6. Let cool in pan on a wire rack for about 5 minutes, then cut into bars. Remove from pan when cool.

Makes 18 bars.

WHITE-CHOCOLATE BROWNIES

The rich cocoa butter in a bar of white chocolate is the secret of chocolate-chip–dotted brownies of considerable elegance.

- 1 *bar (3 oz) white chocolate*
- ½ *cup butter or margarine*
- 1½ *cups flour*
- ½ *teaspoon baking powder*
- ¼ *teaspoon salt*
- 3 *eggs, at room temperature*
- 1½ *cups sugar*
- 1 *teaspoon vanilla extract*
- 1 *package (6 oz) semisweet or milk-chocolate chips*
- ½ *cup sliced almonds*

1. Preheat oven to 350° F. Combine white chocolate and butter in a small, heavy pan over low heat. Let stand until melted, then stir to blend. Let white-chocolate mixture cool while continuing with step 2.

2. Grease a 9- by 13-inch pan; dust with flour. In a bowl stir together flour, baking powder, and salt to combine thoroughly; set aside.

3. In mixer bowl beat eggs and sugar at high speed until thick and light colored. Blend in vanilla. Gradually add white-chocolate mixture, then flour mixture, beating until well combined. Stir in chocolate chips and ¼ cup of the almonds.

4. Spread batter in prepared pan, and sprinkle with remaining almonds. Bake until edges pull away from sides of pan and center is nearly set when tested with a toothpick (25 to 30 minutes).

5. Let cool in pan on a wire rack for about 10 minutes, then cut into bars. Remove from pan when cool.

Makes 3 dozen bars.

CHOCOLATE–BROWN-SUGAR BROWNIES

For those who like a somewhat milder chocolate flavor, these glossy-crusted brownies with semisweet chocolate and a generous measure of brown sugar are made-to-order.

- ½ *cup butter or margarine*
- 3 *squares (3 oz) semisweet baking chocolate, coarsely chopped*
- 1 *cup flour*
- ¼ *teaspoon baking soda*
- 1½ *cups firmly packed brown sugar*
- ½ *teaspoon vanilla extract*
- 2 *eggs*
- 1 *cup chopped walnuts*

1. Place butter in a 9-inch-square pan to melt as oven preheats to 350° F. Remove pan as soon as butter melts, and set pan with butter aside.

2. Whirl chocolate in food processor or blender until powdery; transfer to a large bowl.

3. To chocolate add flour, baking soda, and brown sugar; stir to combine thoroughly. Add melted butter, vanilla, and eggs; beat with an electric mixer until smooth and glossy (3 to 5 minutes). Stir in walnuts.

4. Spread batter in pan in which butter melted. Bake until a toothpick inserted in center comes out with just a few clinging crumbs (35 to 40 minutes).

5. Let cool in pan on a wire rack for about 10 minutes, then cut into bars. Remove from pan when cool.

Makes 18 bars.

QUICK, EASY BARS

Bar cookies are a convenient choice when you want to make a lot of cookies without spending hours baking. The cookies in this group are the speediest of the lot; they can be put together in a minimum of time, yet offer maximum pleasure.

FOOD-PROCESSOR DATE BARS

Chopping dates and pecans in a food processor and then whirling together the batter make light work of these moist, fruited bars. They keep well and are a good choice to send away to school or camp.

- 2 *cups pitted dates*
- 1 *cup pecans*
- ½ *cup each flour and granulated sugar*
- ½ *teaspoon baking powder*
- ¼ *cup firm butter, diced*
- 1 *egg*
- 2 *egg yolks*
- 1½ *teaspoons vanilla extract Confectioners' sugar*

1. Preheat oven to 350° F. Grease an 8-inch-square pan; dust with flour.

2. In food processor combine dates, pecans, flour, granulated sugar, baking powder, and butter. Process, using short on-off bursts, until dates and nuts are finely chopped.

3. In a small bowl beat egg, egg yolks, and vanilla just enough to blend. With motor running, add egg mixture through feed tube all at once. Process just until all ingredients are well coated with egg mixture. Spread evenly in prepared pan.

4. Bake until top is golden brown (25 to 30 minutes). Let cool in pan on a wire rack for about 10 minutes, then cut into bars. Remove from pan and turn lightly in confectioners' sugar to coat each bar on all sides.

Makes 2 dozen bars.

CHOCOLATE-ALMOND COOKIE BARK

Baked in a large pan, then broken into irregular pieces, these rich, buttery chocolate-chip cookies are as delicious as they are easy to make.

- ¾ *cup butter or margarine, softened*
- ⅓ *cup each granulated sugar and firmly packed light brown sugar*
- 2 *tablespoons coffee-flavored liqueur*
- 1½ *cups flour*
- 1 *package (6 oz) semisweet chocolate chips*
- ½ *cup slivered almonds*

1. Preheat oven to 375° F.

2. In large mixer bowl combine butter and sugars; beat until light and fluffy. Gradually blend in coffee liqueur.

3. Gradually add flour, mixing until blended. Stir in chocolate chips.

4. Spread mixture evenly in an ungreased, shallow, 10- by 15-inch pan. Sprinkle evenly with almonds, pressing them lightly into dough.

5. Bake until cookies are well browned (18 to 20 minutes). Cool completely in pan on a wire rack, then turn out and break into irregularly shaped pieces.

Makes about 4 dozen cookies.

Chocolate-Cherry Cookie Pizza is baked in a pizza pan, then cut into cookie-sized wedges. It's sure to be the hit of the slumber party.

CHOCOLATE-CHERRY COOKIE PIZZA

Use a pizza pan to bake this giant, sugar-dusted cookie. Then cut it into pizza-shaped wedges.

  ½ cup butter or margarine, softened
  ½ cup firmly packed brown sugar
  1 teaspoon vanilla extract
  1 cup flour
  1 cup coarsely chopped semisweet chocolate
  ½ cup coarsely chopped pecans
  ⅓ cup red candied cherries, halved
  Confectioners' sugar

1. Preheat oven to 375° F.

2. In large mixer bowl beat butter and brown sugar until light and fluffy; blend in vanilla. Gradually add flour, mixing until blended. Stir in chocolate, pecans, and cherries.

3. Pat mixture evenly over surface of a lightly greased, flat, 11- to 12-inch-diameter pizza pan (dough will be thick; use your fingers if necessary), spreading nearly to outer edge of pan.

4. Bake until well browned (14 to 16 minutes). Cool for 10 minutes in pan on wire rack, then use a pizza cutter or knife to cut into wedges. Sprinkle lightly with confectioners' sugar. Remove from pan when cool.

Makes 18 wedge-shaped cookies.

EASY DATE-ORANGE BARS

This is an easy, all-in-one-saucepan bar cookie. If you enlist some help in chopping nuts and cutting up dates, the cookie batter can be readied for the oven in minutes.

  1 cup flour
  ½ teaspoon baking soda
  ½ cup butter or margarine
  ½ cup sugar
  1 teaspoon grated orange rind
  2 tablespoons orange juice
  1 egg
  ½ cup chopped walnuts
  ½ cup chopped pitted dates
  Confectioners' sugar

1. In a bowl stir together flour and baking soda to combine thoroughly; set aside.

2. Preheat oven to 350° F. Lightly grease an 8-inch-square pan.

3. Place butter in a 2-quart saucepan over medium heat until melted. Remove pan from heat. Add sugar, orange rind, and orange juice. Mix until blended thoroughly. Beat in egg. Then add flour mixture and beat just until batter is well combined. Stir in walnuts and dates. Spread batter in prepared pan.

4. Bake until edges begin to pull away from sides of pan and a toothpick inserted in center comes out clean (25 to 30 minutes).

5. Let stand in pan on a wire rack for about 10 minutes. Cut into bars and sift confectioners' sugar over them. Remove from pan when cool.

Makes 18 bars.

FRAGRANT VANILLA SUGAR

Vanilla is a magical flavor that seems to heighten and emphasize other flavors. The most familiar form of vanilla is the little brown bottle of extract.

However, by using an aromatic vanilla bean, you can create versatile vanilla sugars to sprinkle on cookies. The flavor is so sophisticated, one wonders how vanilla ever came to be considered "plain."

Many of the recipes in this cookbook call for vanilla sugar in small amounts. Made with either granulated or confectioners' sugar, vanilla sugar can also be used in place of plain sugar in a recipe. In addition, you can use it to sprinkle over berries and other fruits and to flavor whipped cream.

Vanilla Granulated Sugar Split a vanilla bean in half lengthwise. Place both halves in a tall jar. Fill jar with 1 to 2 cups granulated sugar. Cover and let stand for at least 24 hours for sugar to absorb vanilla flavor. Replenish sugar as you use it. Vanilla will continue to flavor sugar for up to a year.

Stirring may dislodge some of the tiny seeds inside the split vanilla bean. They're a potent flavor as they become distributed throughout the sugar. If these tiny specks become too numerous, strain sugar through a fine sieve as you use it, returning seeds to sugar in jar.

Vanilla Confectioners' Sugar Substitute confectioners' sugar for granulated sugar in the directions given above.

These bars are made with (left to right) apricots and almonds, chocolate and pecans, poppy seed, and chocolate and almonds (see pages 44 and 45).

Although Fresh Lemon Bars have a flavor as carefree as springtime, they can be baked during any month of the year.

LAYERED BARS

The cookies in this group all begin with a bottom layer of shortbreadlike pastry. The ingredients lavished over this foundation include coconut, nuts, tart citrus fillings, chocolate, fruit preserves, and poppy seed.

FRESH LEMON BARS

A classic among cookies, these refreshing bars have a special appeal for lovers of lemon meringue pie. Serve them as the conclusion to a supper that features a hearty main-dish soup.

1 cup butter or margarine, softened
½ cup confectioners' sugar
1 teaspoon vanilla extract
2 cups flour
4 eggs
2 cups granulated sugar
Grated rind of 1 lemon
6 tablespoons lemon juice
¼ cup (approximately) confectioners' sugar, for topping

1. Preheat oven to 350° F. Generously grease a 9- by 13-inch pan.

2. In mixer bowl combine butter, the ½ cup confectioners' sugar, and vanilla; beat until fluffy. Gradually add flour, mixing until well combined. Spread evenly in prepared pan. Bake for 20 minutes.

3. While pastry bakes, in a bowl combine eggs, granulated sugar, lemon rind, and lemon juice; stir to blend all ingredients (do not beat). Pour lemon mixture over baked layer.

4. Return to oven and bake until topping is set and lightly browned (18 to 22 minutes).

5. Sift additional confectioners' sugar over warm cookies to cover top generously. Cut into bars. Remove from pan when cool.

Makes 3 dozen bars.

CHOCOLATE-COCONUT BARS

A vein of soft, melted chocolate separates the vanilla-scented pastry from the generous coconut topping in these three-layered bars.

1 package (6 oz) semisweet or milk-chocolate chips
2 tablespoons flour
½ teaspoon baking powder
¼ teaspoon salt
2 eggs
1 cup firmly packed brown sugar
1 teaspoon vanilla extract
1½ cups flaked coconut

Press-In Pastry

1¼ cups flour
½ cup Vanilla Confectioners' Sugar (see page 39)
½ cup firm butter or margarine

1. Preheat oven to 375° F. Prepare Press-In Pastry; press firmly and evenly over bottom of an ungreased 9- by 13-inch baking pan. Bake for 10 minutes.

2. Remove pan from oven and sprinkle chocolate chips evenly over hot pastry; set aside.

3. In a small bowl stir together flour, baking powder, and salt to combine thoroughly; set aside. In mixer bowl beat eggs and brown sugar at high speed until thick; blend in vanilla. Stir in flour mixture, then coconut. Spread evenly over chocolate chips.

4. Return to oven and bake until top is well browned and springs back when touched lightly (15 to 20 minutes). Let stand in pan on a wire rack for about 10 minutes, then cut into bars. Remove from pan when cool.

Makes 3 dozen bars.

Press-In Pastry

1. In a medium-sized bowl stir together flour and Vanilla Confectioners' Sugar to combine thoroughly.

2. Using a pastry blender or 2 knives, cut in butter until mixture forms coarse crumbs.

Tips

BAR COOKIES À LA MODE

As every student of sweets has observed, an almost foolproof way to make a tempting dessert even better is to scoop ice cream on top of it. Brownies and other bar cookies are no exception—especially if the cookies are just baked and warm from the oven.

When you make bar cookies to serve in this manner, you can cut them about twice as large as the recipe specifies.

Most of these dessert cookies can be baked in short order. Yet dinner guests will give you credit for having worked on the dessert for hours.

If you need suggestions for combining bar cookies and ice cream, try these for a start.

☐ Classic Fudge Brownies (see page 32) with rich vanilla ice cream and fresh raspberries

☐ Espresso Brownies (see page 32) with coffee ice cream

☐ Butterscotch Saucepan Brownies (see page 32) with butter-pecan ice cream

☐ Swedish Almond Brownies (see page 32) with mocha-almond-fudge ice cream

☐ Easy Date-Orange Bars (see page 39) with orange sherbet

☐ Chocolate-Coconut Bars (left) with fudge-ripple ice cream

☐ Apricot-Almond Squares (see page 44) with toasted-almond ice cream

☐ Ginger-Glazed Spiced Shortbread (see page 50) with peach sorbet

LAYERED ORANGE BARS

This standard bar-cookie recipe has several irresistible variations. In addition to the basic orange-accented version, you will want to try lemony Dream Bars and eye-catching Chocolate-Drizzled Pecan Bars.

    ¼ cup flour
    ½ teaspoon baking powder
    2 eggs
    1 cup firmly packed
       brown sugar
    1 teaspoon vanilla extract
    1 tablespoon grated
       orange rind
    1 cup chopped walnuts
    1½ cups flaked coconut

Orange Pastry

    ½ cup butter or margarine,
       softened
    ½ cup granulated sugar
    1 teaspoon grated orange rind
    1 cup flour

Orange Glaze

    1 cup confectioners' sugar
    1 teaspoon grated orange rind
    1½ tablespoons orange juice

1. Preheat oven to 375° F. Prepare Orange Pastry; press firmly and evenly over bottom of a greased 9- by 13-inch baking pan. Bake for 10 minutes, then remove pastry from oven. Reduce temperature to 350° F.

2. In a small bowl combine flour and baking powder; stir to combine thoroughly. In mixer bowl combine eggs and brown sugar; beat until well mixed. Blend in vanilla and orange rind. Gradually beat in flour mixture until well combined. Stir in walnuts and coconut. Spread mixture over partially baked pastry.

3. Bake until well browned and set in center (20 to 25 minutes). Remove pan to a rack; drizzle with glaze while warm. Let stand until glaze is set, then cut into bars. Remove from pan when cool.

Makes 3 dozen bars.

Orange Pastry In mixer bowl combine butter, sugar, and orange rind; beat until fluffy. Gradually stir in flour until mixture is well combined (dough will be crumbly).

Orange Glaze Combine confectioners' sugar and orange rind in a small bowl; stir in orange juice until icing is smooth.

Dream Bars Omit orange rind from filling; substitute chopped pecans for walnuts. Omit orange rind from pastry; substitute firmly packed brown sugar for granulated sugar. Omit orange rind and juice from glaze; substitute lemon rind and juice.

Chocolate-Drizzled Pecan Bars
Omit orange rind from filling; substitute chopped pecans for walnuts. Increase vanilla to 1½ teaspoons. Omit orange rind from pastry; substitute ½ teaspoon vanilla. Omit glaze. While cookies are cooling, melt 1 square (1 oz) semisweet baking chocolate with ½ teaspoon salad oil in a small, heavy pan over low heat. Drizzle melted chocolate over baked cookies from a paper cone (see page 109) or the tip of a teaspoon. Cut into bars after chocolate sets.

APRICOT-ALMOND SQUARES

A crisply toasted almond pastry and a tart, moist apricot filling characterize these elegant bar cookies.

    1 cup dried apricots
    ½ cup unblanched almonds
    ½ cup butter or margarine,
       softened
    ¼ cup granulated sugar
    1 cup flour
    ½ teaspoon baking powder
    ¼ teaspoon salt
    2 eggs, at room temperature
    1 cup firmly packed
       brown sugar
    ½ teaspoon vanilla extract
    ¼ teaspoon almond extract
       Confectioners' sugar

1. Preheat oven to 350° F. Place apricots in a small saucepan; cover with water. Bring to a boil over medium-high heat. Cover and simmer until tender (6 to 8 minutes). Drain and pat dry with paper towels. Cut into thin slivers and set aside.

2. Spread almonds in a shallow pan. Bake until toasted (8 to 10 minutes). Let cool; whirl in blender or food processor to form coarse crumbs.

3. In mixer bowl combine butter and granulated sugar; beat until fluffy. Blend in ½ cup of the flour and ground almonds. Spread mixture evenly over bottom of an ungreased, 9-inch-square baking pan. Bake for 20 minutes; remove pan from oven.

4. While pastry is baking, in a small bowl stir together remaining ½ cup flour, baking powder, and salt to combine thoroughly; set aside.

5. In mixer bowl beat eggs and brown sugar at high speed until thick. Gradually blend in flour mixture, then vanilla and almond extracts. Stir in apricots. Spread over baked layer.

6. Return to oven and bake until well browned (about 30 minutes). Cool about 10 minutes, then cut into squares. Sift lightly with confectioners' sugar. Remove from pan when cool.

Makes 3 dozen squares.

GERMAN ALMOND-CHOCOLATE BARS

German pastry bakers are justly celebrated for their sumptuous tortes, lavish with almonds, chocolate, and butter. In lighter moments, they use many of the same ingredients to confect cookies that are nearly as impressive. These chocolate-glazed bars come from the ancient Moselle River town of Trier.

1 cup blanched almonds
2 tablespoons flour
½ teaspoon ground cinnamon
½ cup butter or margarine, softened
¾ cup sugar
½ teaspoon vanilla extract
¾ teaspoon almond extract
3 eggs
2 squares (2 oz) semisweet chocolate, grated

Almond Press-In Pastry

¾ cup flour
⅓ cup confectioners' sugar
¼ cup firm butter or margarine
1 egg yolk
½ teaspoon almond extract

1. Preheat oven to 350° F. Spread almonds in a shallow pan. Bake until toasted (8 to 10 minutes). Let cool, then whirl in blender or food processor to form coarse crumbs.

2. Prepare Almond Press-In Pastry; press firmly and evenly into bottom of a lightly greased, 8-inch-square baking pan. Bake until lightly browned (10 to 12 minutes). Remove from oven and place pan on a wire rack while preparing almond mixture.

3. In a small bowl stir together flour and cinnamon to combine thoroughly; set aside. In mixer bowl beat butter and sugar until fluffy. Blend in vanilla and almond extracts, then almonds. Add eggs, one at a time, beating well after each addition. Add flour mixture and blend well.

4. Spread almond mixture over lightly browned pastry. Return to oven and bake until top is well browned and set in center when tested with a toothpick (30 to 35 minutes).

5. Sprinkle grated chocolate evenly over hot surface of just-baked cookies. Let stand in pan on a wire rack for about 20 minutes, then spread soft chocolate over top to form a glaze. Cool, then cut into bars and remove from pan.

Makes 2 dozen bars.

Almond Press-In Pastry

1. In a medium bowl stir together flour and confectioners' sugar to combine thoroughly. Using a pastry blender or 2 knives, cut in butter until mixture forms coarse crumbs.

2. In a small bowl beat egg yolk with almond extract; add mixture to pastry and stir until just combined.

FILLED POPPY-SEED BARS

From the same Trier *Konditorei* that creates German Almond-Chocolate Bars comes the inspiration for sugar-dusted bars with a moist, poppy-seed filling.

¾ cup poppy seed
¼ cup blanched almonds
½ cup granulated sugar
¼ teaspoon ground nutmeg
⅓ cup milk
½ teaspoon grated lemon rind
2 teaspoons lemon juice
2 tablespoons butter or margarine
Confectioners' sugar

Cookie Crust and Crumbly Topping

¼ cup blanched almonds
1 cup flour
½ cup confectioners' sugar
1 teaspoon baking powder
½ cup firm butter or margarine
1 egg yolk
½ teaspoon vanilla extract

1. In blender or food processor, combine poppy seed and almonds; whirl until powdery. Transfer mixture to a 1½- to 2-quart saucepan, and add granulated sugar, nutmeg, milk, lemon rind, lemon juice, and butter. Place over medium heat; cook, stirring often, until mixture boils and thickens (about 10 minutes). Remove from heat and set aside.

2. Prepare Cookie Crust and Crumbly Topping. Preheat oven to 350° F.

3. Press half of crust mixture evenly and firmly over bottom of an ungreased, 8-inch-square baking pan. Spread poppy-seed mixture evenly over crust. Sprinkle remaining crust mixture over filling in coarse, irregular particles.

4. Bake until topping is well browned (30 to 35 minutes). Cool in pan on a rack for about 20 minutes, then cut into bars. Sift with confectioners' sugar. Remove cookies from pan when completely cool.

Makes 2 dozen bars.

Cookie Crust and Crumbly Topping

1. Place almonds in blender or food processor and whirl until a fine powder forms.

2. In a large bowl stir together flour, confectioners' sugar, and baking powder until thoroughly combined. Add ground almonds and stir until blended.

3. Using a pastry blender or 2 knives, cut in butter until mixture forms coarse crumbs.

4. In a small bowl beat egg yolk with vanilla. Add egg-vanilla mixture to flour-almond mixture and stir until just combined. Divide pastry into 2 equal parts.

Baked in strips, then cut apart, are (top to bottom) Spiced Prune Bars, Strawberry-Filled Butter Slices, and Hermits (see pages 48 and 49).

COOKIES TO KEEP

Although a cookie jar is the obvious place to store cookies, wonderful cookies tend to disappear long before they begin to grow stale.

However, if you have a surplus—or if you are thinking ahead—you may be interested in ways to keep cookies fresh and delicious.

☐ If you are storing more than one kind of cookie, keep them separate. If placed together, crisp cookies will absorb moisture from soft, cakelike cookies; before long all will be soggy.

☐ If cookies have icing or another topping, separate successive layers with sheets of waxed paper.

☐ Cookies kept for short periods of time (up to a week) are best stored in a tightly covered tin at room temperature. Be sure the cookies have cooled completely before packing them in a container.

☐ Cookies stored for longer periods of time (up to 3 or 4 months) can be kept in the freezer. Package each kind of cookie separately in an airtight enclosure of freezer wrap, freezer-weight plastic bags, heavy aluminum foil, or a foil-lined container.

☐ Rich, buttery, crisp cookies tend to freeze better than soft, moist, cakelike ones. Brownies are the exception; they can be frozen with great success.

☐ Thaw frozen cookies in their freezer wrapping or container at room temperature for 15 to 30 minutes. If cookies need frosting, glazing, or sprinkling with sugar, wait until they are completely thawed to add it.

SLICE-APART STRIPS

Bar cookies usually take their form from the square or rectangular pan in which they bake. But there is another way to create bar-shaped cookies. Using two spatulas to spread the fairly stiff dough, form long, narrow strips the length of a baking sheet, allowing room for the cookies to spread sideways during baking. While the baked cookies are still warm enough to cut easily, slice each strip crosswise into bars. This way you can produce quantities of cookies in record time.

STRAWBERRY-FILLED BUTTER SLICES

As festive in looks as they are in flavor, these tender butter cookies are good to serve as a sweet with tea.

> 1⅔ cups flour
> ½ teaspoon baking soda
> ¼ teaspoon salt
> ½ cup butter or margarine, softened
> ¾ cup confectioners' sugar
> 1 egg
> 1 teaspoon vanilla extract
> ½ cup finely chopped unblanched hazelnuts, or walnuts
> ½ cup strawberry preserves
>   Confectioners' sugar (optional)

1. In a bowl stir together flour, baking soda, and salt to combine thoroughly; set aside.

2. Preheat oven to 350° F. In mixer bowl combine butter and the ¾ cup confectioners' sugar; beat until fluffy and well combined. Beat in egg until fluffy. Blend in vanilla.

3. Gradually add flour mixture, then hazelnuts, blending until well combined.

4. Using a third of the dough for each strip, spread dough in 1½-inch-wide, ½-inch-thick strips, about 2 inches apart, down the length of greased baking sheets. With your floured finger or teaspoon, make a ½-inch-wide depression down the entire length of the center of each strip.

5. Bake for 5 minutes, then remove from oven and press depressions down again. Return cookies to oven and bake until golden brown (10 to 12 minutes).

6. Fill depressions in warm cookie strips with preserves. Let cool on baking sheets for about 15 minutes, then cut, slightly on the diagonal, into 1-inch-wide bars. Sift lightly with confectioners' sugar, if desired.

Makes about 42 cookies.

HERMITS

Traditional, spicy Hermits, chock-full of raisins and nuts, are at their best the day they are baked, when they are crisp on the outside and moist inside.

> 3⅓ cups flour
> 1 teaspoon each *ground cinnamon and ground ginger*
> ½ teaspoon each *salt, ground nutmeg, and ground cloves*
> ½ cup *vegetable shortening*
> ½ cup *butter or margarine, softened*
> ½ cup each *granulated sugar and firmly packed brown sugar*
> 2 eggs
> ½ cup *light molasses*
> 1 teaspoon *baking soda, dissolved in ¼ cup warm water*
> 1 cup each *dark raisins, golden raisins, and chopped walnuts*

1. In a bowl stir together flour, cinnamon, ginger, salt, nutmeg, and cloves to combine well; set aside.

2. Preheat oven to 375° F. In mixer bowl combine shortening, butter, and sugars; beat until fluffy and well blended. Add eggs, one at a time, beating until fluffy after each addition. Blend in molasses.

3. Add flour mixture alternately with baking soda mixture, blending after each addition. Stir in raisins and walnuts.

4. Using about one sixth of the dough for each strip, spread dough in 1½-inch-wide, ¾-inch-thick strips, about 2 inches apart, down the length of greased baking sheets.

5. Bake until a toothpick inserted in center of each strip comes out barely clean (12 to 15 minutes). Let strips stand on baking sheets on a wire rack for about 10 minutes, then cut, slightly on the diagonal, into 1-inch-wide bars.

Makes about 66 bars.

SPICED PRUNE BARS

Moist and chewy with prunes, these lemon-glazed cookie strips are encrusted with crisp, chopped walnuts. Select moist-packed pitted prunes for these cookies. Their soft texture makes the strips easier to slice after they have been baked and glazed.

> *2 cups flour*
> *1 teaspoon ground cinnamon*
> *½ teaspoon baking soda*
> *¼ teaspoon salt*
> *¼ teaspoon ground nutmeg*
> *⅛ teaspoon ground cloves*
> *1 cup chopped pitted prunes*
> *½ cup butter or margarine, softened*
> *1 cup firmly packed dark brown sugar*
> *1 egg*
> *1 cup finely chopped walnuts*

Lemon Glaze

> *¾ cup confectioners' sugar*
> *¼ teaspoon grated lemon rind*
> *1 to 1½ tablespoons lemon juice*

1. In a bowl stir together flour, cinnamon, baking soda, salt, nutmeg, and cloves to combine thoroughly. Add prunes, stirring to coat well with flour mixture.

2. Preheat oven to 375° F. Place butter and brown sugar in a mixer bowl and beat until well combined. Beat in egg until mixture is fluffy.

3. Gradually blend in flour mixture. Divide dough into 4 equal portions.

4. Spread walnuts on a large piece of waxed paper. Shape each portion of dough into a long roll and turn in nuts to coat well on all sides.

5. Transfer nut-encrusted rolls to greased baking sheets. Flatten rolls into strips with your fingertips until they are about 1½ inches wide and ¾ inch thick. Sprinkle strips with any remaining nuts.

6. Bake until a toothpick inserted in center of each strip comes out clean and nuts are toasted (15 to 20 minutes). Let cool on baking sheets for 10 minutes.

7. Drizzle strips with Lemon Glaze. Then cut, slightly on the diagonal, into 1-inch-wide bars. Transfer bars to wire racks to cool completely.

Makes about 4 dozen cookies.

Lemon Glaze In a small bowl combine confectioners' sugar and lemon rind. Gradually add lemon juice, stirring until glaze is smooth and of a good drizzling consistency.

Tips

COOKIES TO SEND

A package of cookies from home is a welcome gift to youngsters away at camp or to older offspring in college or the military. To avoid crumbled cookies (and the wry remarks occasioned by such a catastrophe), heed these suggestions.

☐ Choose cookies that can take jostling. Very thin, crisp cookies may not endure the strain. Most bar cookies—except shortbread—and the oatmeal cookies on pages 18 through 20 are good travelers.

☐ Moist-textured cookies usually retain their freshness well, so they are a good choice to send if a package needs several days to reach its destination.

☐ If you send both crisp and soft cookies together, wrap them separately so each kind will retain its own texture.

☐ Pack cookies in a sturdy container. Fill the bottom with an even layer of something to cushion the cookies, such as crumpled paper, plain popcorn, bubble plastic wrap, or Styrofoam packing material. Then arrange cookies as tightly together as possible in each layer, separating layers with waxed paper or aluminum foil. Fill crevices between cookies with popcorn. An alternative is to wrap individual cookies in pairs (flat sides together) using plastic wrap. Enclose bar cookies in layers the size of the mailing container. Use sheets of Styrofoam packing material or loose Styrofoam packing pellets to fill all spaces snugly. Seal the package with mailing tape and ship to arrive as quickly as possible.

SHORTBREAD

The word *short* has a number of meanings. When the subject is cookies, it means crisp and tender, due to an abundance of butter. Whether the unembellished splendor of the Scotch original or one of many possible flavored versions, all shortbread cookies share a sandy-textured richness that is hard to resist.

CHOCOLATE-PECAN SHORTBREAD

Use a Dutch-process cocoa to give these very thin, very crisp cookies the boldest possible chocolate flavor.

> 1 *cup flour*
> ¼ *cup each unsweetened cocoa and finely chopped pecans*
> ⅛ *teaspoon each baking soda and salt*
> ½ *cup butter or margarine, softened*
> ⅔ *cup confectioners' sugar*
> 1 *teaspoon vanilla extract*

1. Preheat oven to 325° F. Lightly grease a 9-inch-square baking pan; dust with flour.

2. In a bowl stir together flour, cocoa, pecans, baking soda, and salt to combine thoroughly; set aside.

3. In mixer bowl combine butter and confectioners' sugar; beat until fluffy and well mixed. Blend in vanilla. Gradually add flour mixture until it is completely absorbed (dough will be crumbly).

4. Pat dough evenly and firmly into a smooth layer in prepared pan. Bake until top feels firm when touched gently and edges pull away from sides of pan (30 to 35 minutes).

5. Let cool in pan on a wire rack for about 10 minutes, then cut into bars. Remove from pan when cool.

Makes 2 dozen bars.

CLASSIC SCOTCH SHORTBREAD

Thin, crisp, and meltingly tender, these traditional cookies are not overly sweet. If you prefer a sweeter flavor, sift an additional tablespoon of the Vanilla Confectioners' Sugar over the cookies after you cut them into wedges.

> 1 *cup flour*
> 6 *tablespoons Vanilla Confectioners' Sugar (see page 39)*
> ½ *cup firm butter or margarine, diced*

1. Preheat oven to 325° F. In a medium bowl stir together flour and Vanilla Confectioners' Sugar to combine thoroughly.

2. Using a pastry blender or your fingers, cut or crumble in butter until all the particles are uniformly small and well coated with flour mixture. Use your hands to firmly press crumbly dough into a flattened ball.

3. Place dough in an ungreased 8-inch-diameter pan, preferably with a removable bottom. Press dough evenly and firmly into pan. Use your index finger to impress a row of uniformly spaced dimples around outer edge. With tines of a fork, score dough into 12 wedges; then pierce randomly between scores to keep cookies flat.

4. Bake until color is pale golden brown (30 to 35 minutes). Remove pan from oven and place on a rack to cool for about 10 minutes. Cut cookies into wedges along previous scorings. When cool, remove pan sides and cookies.

Makes 1 dozen cookies.

GINGER-GLAZED SPICED SHORTBREAD

The dominant flavor of these crisp bar cookies is ginger, but cinnamon and cloves add intriguing complexity. Serve them with a fresh fruit sorbet.

> 1¼ *cups flour*
> 1 *teaspoon each baking powder and ground ginger*
> ½ *teaspoon ground cinnamon*
> ¼ *teaspoon ground cloves*
> ½ *cup butter or margarine, softened*
> ½ *cup sugar*

Ginger Glaze

> 2 *tablespoons butter or margarine*
> 1 *teaspoon ground ginger*
> ¼ *cup confectioners' sugar*
> 2 *teaspoons light corn syrup*

1. Preheat oven to 350° F. Lightly grease a 9-inch-square baking pan; dust with flour.

2. In a bowl stir together flour, baking powder, ginger, cinnamon, and cloves to combine thoroughly; set aside.

3. In mixer bowl combine butter and sugar; beat until fluffy and well blended. Gradually add flour mixture until well combined (dough will be crumbly).

4. Pat dough evenly and firmly into a smooth layer in prepared pan. Bake until top browns lightly and edges pull away from sides of pan (25 to 30 minutes).

5. Let cool in pan on a wire rack for 5 minutes, then spread with warm Ginger Glaze. Cut into bars. Remove from pan when cool.

Makes 2 dozen bars.

Ginger Glaze While cookies are cooling, melt butter in a small pan over low heat. Stir in ginger, then confectioners' sugar and corn syrup until mixture is smooth. Remove pan from heat.

BROWN-SUGAR SHORTBREAD

The intense butterscotch flavor of these crisp, triangular cookies makes them a delightful complement to fresh raspberries.

- ½ cup butter or margarine, softened
- ⅔ cup firmly packed dark brown sugar
- ½ teaspoon vanilla extract
- 1¼ cups flour

1. Preheat oven to 325° F. Lightly grease a 9-inch-square baking pan; dust with flour.

2. In mixer bowl combine butter and brown sugar; beat until fluffy and well mixed. Blend in vanilla. Gradually add flour until it is completely absorbed (dough will be stiff).

3. Pat dough evenly and firmly into a smooth layer in prepared pan. Bake until top feels firm when touched gently and edges pull away from sides of pan (30 to 35 minutes).

4. Let cool in pan on a wire rack for about 10 minutes. Cut into 16 squares; then cut each in half to make 2 triangles. Remove from pan when cool.

Makes 32 cookies.

Crisp Brown-Sugar Shortbread cookies, cut into triangles while still slightly warm, make an elegant dessert with fresh berries or your choice of ice cream.

TWICE-BAKED ITALIAN COOKIES

In Italy the practice of dunking has been raised to something approaching an art. Not with doughnuts, of course, but with cookies. They're baked twice—hence the name, *biscotti*—to be sure they will be crisp, hard, and dry enough to absorb a maximum amount of moisture without crumbling away.

The beverage of choice might be espresso coffee of almost impenetrable blackness. Wine is another possibility, be it the last of the local red left in the glass at the end of a meal or a slightly sweet wine such as Sagrantino, selected to complement cheese and fruit for dessert.

CANDIED FRUIT SLICES

There is a tendency in the United States to associate candied fruit with holiday baking, but that distinction is taken less seriously in Italy. Although these almond-and-fruit cookie slices are colorful enough to serve for Christmas, they can be appreciated the year around.

  2½ *cups flour*
  1½ *teaspoons baking powder*
  ¼   *teaspoon salt*
  ¼   *teaspoon anise seed, coarsely crushed*
  ¼   *cup butter or margarine, softened*
  1   *cup granulated sugar*
  1   *teaspoon vanilla extract*
  2   *teaspoons grated orange rind*
  3   *eggs*
  1   *cup unblanched whole almonds*
  ½   *cup mixed candied fruit*
  ¼   *cup red candied cherries*
  1   *tablespoon (approximately) coarse sugar (pearl or decorating sugar, or crushed sugar cubes), optional*

1. In a medium bowl stir together flour, baking powder, salt, and anise seed to combine thoroughly; set aside.

2. In mixer bowl combine butter and the 1 cup granulated sugar; beat until well mixed. Blend in vanilla and orange rind. Separate 1 egg, reserving white in a small bowl. To butter mixture add egg yolk, then remaining 2 eggs, one at a time, beating well after each addition.

3. Gradually beat in flour mixture until dough is smooth and well blended. Divide dough in half and enclose each portion in plastic wrap. Refrigerate until firm (about 1 hour).

4. While dough is chilling, combine almonds, mixed candied fruit, and candied cherries.

5. Preheat oven to 350° F. On a lightly floured surface, roll out 1 portion of dough to an 8- by 12-inch rectangle. Sprinkle with half of fruit mixture. Starting with a 12-inch edge, roll rectangle compactly, jelly-roll style. Pinch edge and ends to seal. Place, sealed side down, on a lightly greased baking sheet. Repeat with other portion of dough.

6. Beat reserved egg white until slightly bubbly; brush egg white over each roll. Sprinkle rolls lightly with coarse sugar (if desired.)

7. Bake until golden brown (35 to 40 minutes). Let rolls cool on baking sheet on a wire rack for about 5 minutes.

8. Transfer rolls to a board; with a serrated knife cut rolls on the diagonal into ½-inch-thick slices. Place slices, cut sides down, on baking sheets and return to oven. Bake until crisply toasted (15 to 20 minutes). Transfer to wire racks to cool completely.

Makes about 4 dozen cookies.

SPICED NUT COOKIES

Made in the same manner as the cookies in the previous recipe, these *biscotti*, known in Italy as *quaresimali*, are generously spiced and studded with hazelnuts, walnuts, and pine nuts. Because these cookies are baked to the dryness of a rusk, they keep well for weeks. Store them in a tightly covered tin so you can enjoy them whenever your cup or glass holds a few last swallows for dunking.

  2½ *cups flour*
  1½ *teaspoons baking powder*
  1   *teaspoon ground cinnamon*
  ½   *teaspoon ground nutmeg*
  ¼   *teaspoon each salt and ground allspice*
  ¼   *cup butter or margarine, softened*
  1   *cup sugar, plus sugar for sprinkling*
  1   *teaspoon vanilla extract*
  3   *eggs*
  1   *cup each unblanched whole hazelnuts or almonds and coarsely chopped walnuts*
  ⅓   *cup pine nuts*

1. In a medium bowl stir together flour, baking powder, cinnamon, nutmeg, salt, and allspice to combine thoroughly; set aside.

2. In a mixer bowl combine butter and the 1 cup sugar; beat until well mixed. Blend in vanilla. Separate 1 egg, reserving white in a small bowl. To butter mixture add egg yolk, then remaining 2 eggs, one at a time, beating well after each addition.

3. Gradually beat flour mixture into butter mixture until dough is smooth and well blended. Divide dough in half and enclose each portion in plastic wrap. Refrigerate until firm (about 1 hour).

4. While dough is chilling, stir hazelnuts, walnuts, and pine nuts together in a small bowl.

5. Preheat oven to 350° F. On a lightly floured surface, roll out 1 portion of dough to an 8- by 12-inch rectangle. Sprinkle with half of nut mixture. Starting with a 12-inch side, roll rectangle compactly, jelly-roll style. Pinch edge and ends to seal. Place, sealed side down, on a lightly greased baking sheet. Repeat with other portion of dough.

6. In a small bowl beat reserved egg white until slightly bubbly; brush egg white over each roll. Sprinkle rolls lightly with sugar.

7. Bake until golden brown (35 to 40 minutes). Let rolls cool on baking sheet on a wire rack for about 5 minutes.

8. Transfer rolls to a board; with a serrated knife cut rolls on the diagonal into ½-inch-thick slices. Place slices, cut sides down, on baking sheets and return to oven. Bake until crisply toasted (15 to 20 minutes). Transfer to wire racks to cool completely.

Makes about 4 dozen cookies.

Sugar-sprinkled Chocolate Pretzels are one of the more elaborate forms into which buttery cookies can be molded. The recipe is on page 70.

Molded Cookies

The only way to make some of the world's favorite cookies is to get your hands into the dough. When you bake such temptations as Chinese Almond Cookies, old-fashioned Snickerdoodles, Plump Ginger Cookies, or traditional peanut butter cookies, you must shape the rich, buttery dough by hand. The simplest of these cookies are shaped into balls before baking. More intricate variations might be formed into crescents, strands, or twists, or pressed into small muffin pans to make cookies resembling tiny tarts.

SPHERES

The simplest way to shape cookie dough by hand is to mold it into a ball. Although the typically sweet, butter-rich dough used to make molded cookies can withstand a certain amount of handling and still stay tender, these cookies will be best if your touch is light.

SESAME CAKES

Made with vegetable oil, these sesame seed–coated cookies have a moist, slightly cakelike interior. Their sweet, egg flavor and sesame crunch make them a suitable dessert to serve with fruit after an Asian meal.

 2 cups flour
 ½ teaspoon baking powder
 ¼ cup salad oil (such as corn oil)
 3 eggs, at room temperature
 ¾ cup sugar
 ½ teaspoon vanilla extract
 1 cup sesame seed

1. Preheat oven to 350° F.

2. In a large bowl stir together flour and baking powder to combine thoroughly. Make a well in center. Pour oil into well and stir to blend.

3. In mixer bowl combine 2 of the eggs, sugar, and vanilla. Beat at high speed until mixture is thick and light colored. Add egg mixture to flour mixture, beating until thick and well combined.

4. Shape dough into 1-inch balls. In a small bowl beat remaining egg to blend yolk and white. Spread sesame seed in a shallow pan.

5. Dip each cookie into egg to coat lightly, then roll in sesame seed to coat completely. Place cookies about 1½ inches apart on lightly greased baking sheets.

6. Bake until cookies are lightly browned and feel firm when touched gently (15 to 20 minutes). Cool on wire racks.

Makes about thirty 1½-inch cookies.

CHINESE ALMOND COOKIES

When selecting from the varied attractions of certain Chinese take-out restaurants, many people find rich almond cookies, packaged to go in a waxed-paper bag, virtually irresistible. They are just as compelling when baked at home. Making the cookies with a combination of butter and lard brings together the best quality of each ingredient—the flavor of butter and the tender crispness that lard imparts to pastry.

 2 cups flour
 ½ teaspoon baking powder
 ½ cup each butter or margarine and lard, softened
 1 cup sugar
 1 teaspoon almond extract
 ½ teaspoon vanilla extract
 2 egg yolks
 ⅓ cup (approximately) blanched almonds
 2 teaspoons water

1. In a medium-sized bowl stir together flour and baking powder to combine thoroughly; set aside. Preheat oven to 350° F.

2. In mixer bowl combine butter and lard; beat until fluffy. Add sugar and beat until well combined. Blend in almond and vanilla extracts, then 1 egg yolk. Gradually add flour mixture, beating until well combined.

3. Shape dough into 1-inch balls. Place about 1½ inches apart on lightly greased baking sheets. Slightly flatten each cookie with your fingertips; press an almond into center.

4. In a small bowl beat remaining egg yolk with the 2 teaspoons water until blended. Lightly brush top of each cookie with egg-yolk mixture.

5. Bake until cookies are golden brown and feel firm when touched lightly (15 to 18 minutes). Let stand on baking sheets for 1 to 2 minutes, then transfer to wire racks to cool.

Makes about forty-two 2-inch cookies.

Crunchy Sesame Cakes and meltingly tender Chinese Almond Cookies evoke the flavors and textures of Chinese restaurant take-out food.

SNICKERDOODLES

Charmingly old-fashioned, these cookies, covered with cinnamon sugar, recall long afternoons on a porch swing, sipping homemade lemonade.

  1⅓ cups flour
    1 teaspoon cream of tartar
   ½ teaspoon baking soda
   ⅛ teaspoon salt
   ½ cup butter or margarine, softened
   ¾ cup sugar
   ½ teaspoon vanilla extract
    1 egg

Cinnamon Sugar

   ¼ cup sugar
    2 teaspoons ground cinnamon

1. In a bowl stir together flour, cream of tartar, baking soda, and salt to combine thoroughly; set aside. Preheat oven to 400° F.

2. In mixer bowl combine butter and the ¾ cup sugar; beat until fluffy. Blend in vanilla. Beat in egg until well combined. Gradually add flour mixture, beating until just well combined.

3. Drop cookie dough by rounded teaspoons, six to eight at a time, into Cinnamon Sugar spread in a shallow pan. Roll cookies to coat well, shaping them into balls as you roll. Place about 1½ inches apart on greased baking sheets.

4. Bake until edges are golden brown (8 to 10 minutes). Transfer to wire racks to cool.

Makes about 3 dozen 2½-inch cookies.

Cinnamon Sugar In a shallow pan mix sugar and cinnamon until thoroughly combined.

BROWNED BUTTER BALLS

The universal appeal of cookies is exemplified by these delectable morsels of Swedish origin. The ingredients are simple, but they are combined in a distinctive manner. The butter, heated until it is slightly brown, takes on an almost nutty flavor. The texture of the cookies is pleasantly granular.

   ¾ cup butter or margarine
  1½ cups flour
    1 teaspoon baking powder
    1 cup granulated sugar
    2 tablespoons brown sugar
  1½ teaspoons vanilla extract

1. Melt butter in a heavy saucepan over medium heat. Watching carefully, allow butter to heat until it begins to brown. Then pour into mixer bowl and let stand until cooled slightly (about 10 minutes).

2. In a bowl stir together flour and baking powder to combine well; set aside. Preheat oven to 350° F.

3. With electric mixer at high speed, beat butter until lukewarm. Gradually add sugars, beating until mixture is fluffy and light colored. Blend in vanilla.

4. Gradually add flour mixture to butter mixture, beating until dough clings together.

5. Shape dough into 1-inch balls. Place about 1 inch apart on ungreased baking sheets. Bake until lightly browned (18 to 20 minutes). Let stand for 1 to 2 minutes, then transfer to wire racks to cool.

Makes about 3 dozen 1¼-inch cookies.

SHERRY-PECAN BALLS

Flavored with a hint of sherry, these orange-accented butter cookies contain a generous measure of chopped pecans inside and out.

    1 cup flour
  1½ cups finely chopped pecans
   ½ cup butter or margarine, softened
   ½ cup sugar
    2 egg yolks
    1 teaspoon grated orange rind
   ½ teaspoon vanilla extract
    2 tablespoons dry sherry

1. In a bowl stir together flour and ½ cup of the pecans to combine thoroughly; set aside. Spread remaining 1 cup pecans in a shallow pan; set aside.

2. In mixer bowl combine butter and sugar; beat until fluffy. Add egg yolks, one at a time, beating well after each addition. Blend in orange rind and vanilla.

3. To butter mixture add flour mixture alternately with sherry, mixing to blend after each addition. Gather dough into a ball and enclose in plastic wrap. Refrigerate until dough is firm enough to shape (about 45 minutes).

4. Preheat oven to 350° F. Shape dough into 1-inch balls; roll balls in pecans to coat evenly. Place about 1 inch apart on ungreased baking sheets.

5. Bake until cookies are golden brown and feel firm when touched lightly (15 to 20 minutes). Transfer to wire racks to cool.

Makes about 3 dozen 1½-inch cookies.

DATE-WALNUT NUGGETS

There is less cookie here than meets the eye. Concealed inside a cookie coating scented with nutmeg is a walnut-stuffed date. These treats are especially tempting in autumn, when fresh dates and walnuts come to the market.

- 24 pitted dates
- 24 walnut halves
- 1⅓ cups flour
- ⅛ teaspoon each salt and ground nutmeg
- ½ cup finely chopped walnuts
- ½ cup butter or margarine, softened
- ½ cup confectioners' sugar
- 1 teaspoon vanilla extract
- 1 to 2 tablespoons Vanilla Confectioners' Sugar (see page 39)

1. Fill each date with a walnut half, reshaping date around nut; set aside stuffed dates.

2. In a bowl stir together flour, salt, nutmeg, and chopped walnuts to combine thoroughly; set aside. Preheat oven to 350° F.

3. In mixer bowl combine butter and confectioners' sugar; beat until fluffy. Blend in vanilla. Gradually add flour mixture, beating until well combined.

4. Use about 1 tablespoon of dough for each cookie, shaping dough around a stuffed date to cover it evenly. Place dough-wrapped dates about 1½ inches apart on ungreased baking sheets.

5. Bake until cookies are lightly browned and feel firm when touched gently (20 to 25 minutes). Transfer to wire racks. Lightly sift Vanilla Confectioners' Sugar over warm cookies.

Makes 2 dozen 1½-inch cookies.

PLUMP GINGER COOKIES

Ginger and other aromatic spices, molasses, and walnuts combine to fill the kitchen with inviting scents as these jelly-centered cookies bake.

- 2¼ cups flour
- ½ cup ground walnuts
- 1¾ teaspoons baking soda
- ⅛ teaspoon salt
- 1 teaspoon each ground ginger and cinnamon
- ½ teaspoon ground cloves
- ¾ cup butter or margarine, softened
- 1 cup firmly packed brown sugar
- 1 egg
- ¼ cup light molasses
- ¼ cup (approximately) granulated sugar
- 3 to 4 tablespoons red-currant jelly

1. In a bowl stir together flour, walnuts, baking soda, salt, ginger, cinnamon, and cloves to combine thoroughly; set aside. Preheat oven to 350° F.

2. In mixer bowl combine butter and brown sugar; beat until well blended. Beat in egg, then molasses. Gradually add flour mixture, beating until blended.

3. Spread granulated sugar in a shallow pan. Drop cookie dough by heaping tablespoons into sugar. Roll cookies to coat well, shaping them into balls as you roll.

4. Place about 2 inches apart on ungreased baking sheets. With your finger or teaspoon, make a small, deep depression in the center of each cookie. Fill each depression with a rounded ¼ teaspoon jelly.

5. Bake until cookies are brown and feel firm when touched lightly (15 to 18 minutes). Cool on wire racks.

Makes about thirty 2½-inch cookies.

CRISP CHERRY COOKIES

Perky and colorful and with a delicious flavor, these favorite corn flake-coated cookies, in a slightly different form, won a national recipe contest many years ago.

- 1 cup flour
- ½ teaspoon baking powder
- ¼ teaspoon each baking soda and salt
- ½ cup butter or margarine, softened
- 1 cup sugar
- ½ teaspoon vanilla extract
- 1 egg
- ½ cup each chopped walnuts and chopped pitted dates
- ¼ cup chopped maraschino cherries
- 2 cups corn flakes, coarsely crushed
- 18 maraschino cherries, cut into halves

1. In a bowl stir together flour, baking powder, baking soda, and salt to combine thoroughly; set aside. Preheat oven to 375° F.

2. In mixer bowl combine butter and sugar; beat until well blended. Mix in vanilla. Beat in egg until well combined. Gradually add flour mixture, beating until just well blended. Stir in walnuts, dates, and chopped cherries.

3. Spread crushed corn flakes in a shallow pan. Drop cookie dough by level tablespoons, six to eight at a time, into corn flakes. Roll cookies to coat well, shaping them into balls as you roll. Place about 2 inches apart on greased baking sheets. Lightly press a cherry half into center of each cookie.

4. Bake until golden brown (10 to 12 minutes). Cool on wire racks.

Makes 3 dozen 2½-inch cookies.

Pristinely coated with confectioners' sugar and wrapped in crisp, white tissue paper, Mexican Wedding Cakes are given as favors at Oaxacan nuptials.

MEXICAN WEDDING CAKES

Rich with butter and ground nuts, these tender cookies are similar to Greek *kourabiedes* and Austrian *Kipfel*. All three delicacies are coated generously, while still warm, with confectioners' sugar, which seems to melt into the cookies. In the Mexican state of Oaxaca, these cookies are called *bizcochos de boda*. Festively wrapped in fringed white tissue paper, they are given as favors to wedding guests. Serving the cookies in small, fluted paper cups makes them seem similarly festive. For an appealing American variation, the dough can be made with cinnamon and the cookies shaped slightly smaller.

> 2½ cups flour
> ¼ teaspoon salt
> 1 cup finely chopped pecans
> 1 cup butter or margarine, softened
> ½ cup confectioners' sugar
> 2 teaspoons vanilla extract
> 1½ cups (approximately) confectioners' sugar

1. In a bowl stir together flour, salt, and pecans to combine thoroughly; set aside. Preheat oven to 350° F.

2. In mixer bowl combine butter and the ½ cup confectioners' sugar; beat until fluffy. Blend in vanilla. Gradually add flour mixture, beating just until dough clings together.

3. Shape dough into 1½-inch balls. Place about 2 inches apart on ungreased baking sheets. Bake until firm and lightly browned (20 to 25 minutes).

4. Spread about ¾ cup of the remaining confectioners' sugar on a rimmed baking sheet. As cookies finish baking, remove them to sugar-lined baking sheet; generously sift some of the remaining confectioners' sugar over warm cookies, turning in sugar if necessary to coat all surfaces liberally. Transfer to wire racks to complete cooling.

Makes about thirty 1¾-inch cookies.

Cinnamon Balls To flour mixture add 1 teaspoon ground cinnamon. Shape dough into 1-inch balls; place about 1 inch apart on baking sheets. Bake for about 20 minutes.

Makes about forty-two 1¼-inch cookies.

CHOCOLATE CRINKLES

Coating these subtly cinnamon-spiced chocolate cookies with granulated sugar gives them a frosty black-and-white finish. At Christmas decorate these cookies by pressing half of a red candied cherry into the center of each.

> 2 cups flour
> 2 teaspoons baking soda
> 1 teaspoon ground cinnamon
> ¼ teaspoon salt
> ½ cup butter or margarine, softened
> ¼ cup vegetable shortening
> 1¼ cups sugar
> ½ teaspoon vanilla extract
> 1 egg
> ¼ cup light corn syrup
> 2 squares (2 oz) unsweetened chocolate, melted and cooled (see page 10)

1. In a bowl stir together flour, baking soda, cinnamon, and salt to combine thoroughly; set aside. Preheat oven to 350° F.

2. In mixer bowl combine butter and shortening; beat to blend. Add 1 cup of the sugar, beating until fluffy. Add vanilla, then egg, beating until well combined. Blend in corn syrup and chocolate. Gradually add flour mixture, beating until just well combined.

3. Spread remaining ¼ cup sugar in a shallow pan. Shape dough into balls about 1½ inches in diameter. Place balls, six to eight at a time, in pan and roll in sugar to coat lightly on all sides. Place about 2 inches apart on ungreased baking sheets.

4. Bake until cookies feel firm when touched lightly (about 15 minutes). Let cookies stand on baking sheet for about 2 minutes, then transfer to wire racks to cool.

Makes 3 dozen 3-inch cookies.

ALMOND–POPPY-SEED COOKIES

The poppy seed inside these golden orbs and the ground almonds on the outside give these cookies textural variety. They are good with a creamy fruit sherbet.

> ½ cup unblanched almonds
> 2 cups flour
> ¼ teaspoon salt
> 2 tablespoons poppy seed
> 1 cup butter or margarine, softened
> ¾ cup sugar
> 1½ teaspoons vanilla extract
> ½ teaspoon grated lemon rind
> 4 egg yolks

1. Whirl almonds in blender or food processor until they are almost powdery. Spread in a shallow pan and set aside.

2. In a bowl stir together flour, salt, and poppy seed to combine thoroughly; set aside. Preheat oven to 375° F.

3. In mixer bowl beat butter and sugar until fluffy. Blend in vanilla and lemon rind. Add egg yolks, one at a time, beating well after each addition. Gradually add flour mixture, beating until just thoroughly combined.

4. Shape dough into 1-inch balls. Roll in almonds to coat well. Place about 2 inches apart on ungreased baking sheets.

5. Bake until cookies feel firm when touched gently and edges are lightly browned (8 to 10 minutes). Transfer cookies to wire racks to cool.

Makes about forty-two 2-inch cookies.

Eye-fooling coffee bean–shaped chocolate candies accentuate the bittersweet flavor of Coffee Crisps. The recipe is on page 64.

FLATTENED ROUNDS

The cookies in this group are made from dough that has been shaped into balls, then flattened. Depending on the desired effect, the cookies can be flattened with your fingers, the tines of a fork, or a tumbler that has been dipped in sugar.

RUM-PECAN MELTAWAYS

During baking, the surfaces of these sweet, tender cookies take on a crackled texture. When fresh from the oven, the rum flavor is mild. Storing the cookies for a day or two in a covered tin allows the flavor to develop.

- 2 cups flour
- 1 teaspoon baking powder
- ½ teaspoon cream of tartar
- ½ cup butter or margarine, softened
- ¼ cup vegetable shortening
- 2 cups confectioners' sugar
- ½ teaspoon vanilla extract
- 2 tablespoons dark rum
- 1 egg yolk
- ⅔ cup (approximately) pecan halves

1. In a bowl stir together flour, baking powder, and cream of tartar to combine thoroughly; set aside. Preheat oven to 375° F.

2. In mixer bowl combine butter and shortening; beat until fluffy. Add confectioners' sugar and beat until well blended. Stir in vanilla and rum, then egg yolk. Gradually add flour mixture, beating until well combined.

3. Shape dough into 1-inch balls. Place about 1½ inches apart on ungreased baking sheets. Flatten each cookie slightly with your fingertips; press a pecan half into the center.

4. Bake until cookies are lightly browned and feel firm when touched gently (10 to 12 minutes). Let stand for about 2 minutes on baking sheets, then transfer to wire racks to cool.

Makes about forty 2½-inch cookies.

COFFEE CRISPS

The bittersweet coffee flavor of these crunchy cookies is accentuated by placing a coffee bean-shaped chocolate candy in the center of each. Shops selling real coffee beans sometimes offer these sweet imposters.

- 1¾ cups flour
- ¼ teaspoon each *salt, baking soda, and baking powder*
- 1 tablespoon powdered or granulated instant coffee
- ½ cup butter or margarine, softened
- ¼ cup vegetable shortening
- ½ cup each *granulated sugar and firmly packed brown sugar*
- 1½ teaspoons vanilla extract
- 1 egg yolk
- 3 tablespoons (approximately) granulated sugar
- ¼ cup (approximately) coffee bean-shaped chocolate candies

1. In a bowl stir together flour, salt, baking soda, baking powder, and instant coffee to blend thoroughly; set aside. Preheat oven to 375° F.

2. In mixer bowl combine butter and shortening; beat until fluffy. Add sugars and beat until well blended. Beat in vanilla, then egg yolk. Gradually add flour mixture, beating until just well combined.

3. Shape dough into 1-inch balls. Place about 2 inches apart on ungreased baking sheets. Dip a flat-bottomed glass in granulated sugar, and use it to flatten each cookie to a thickness of about ¼ inch. In the center of each cookie, place a coffee bean candy.

4. Bake until cookies are golden brown and feel firm when touched lightly (10 to 12 minutes). Let stand on baking sheets for 1 to 2 minutes, then transfer to wire racks to cool.

Makes about 3 dozen 3-inch cookies.

NORTH GERMAN ALMOND WAFERS

A baked-on glaze of thickened cream and sliced almonds decorates these thin, crisp cookies. The Bremen baker whose cookies inspired this recipe calls his creation a Florida, perhaps because of its flamboyant, cherry-dotted surface.

- 1¾ cups flour
- 2 teaspoons baking powder
- ½ cup butter or margarine, softened
- ½ cup each *granulated sugar and firmly packed brown sugar*
- 1 teaspoon vanilla extract
- 1 egg
- ¼ cup (approximately) granulated sugar
- ¾ cup whipping cream
- 1 tablespoon granulated sugar
- 1 cup sliced almonds
- ¾ cup (approximately) red candied cherries, halved (optional)

1. In a bowl stir together flour and baking powder to blend thoroughly; set aside. Preheat oven to 350° F.

2. In mixer bowl combine butter and the ½ cup each granulated and brown sugars; beat until well blended. Add vanilla, then egg, beating until fluffy. Gradually add flour mixture, beating until well combined.

3. Shape dough into 1-inch balls. Place about 2 inches apart on lightly greased baking sheets. Dip a flat-bottomed glass in the ¼ cup granulated sugar, and use it to flatten each cookie to a thickness of about ¼ inch.

4. In a 1½-quart pan over medium-high heat, combine cream and the 1 tablespoon granulated sugar; bring to a boil. Boil, stirring often, until cream begins to thicken and is reduced by about half (8 to 10 minutes). Remove from heat and stir in almonds. Spoon a scant teaspoon of almond mixture into the center of each cookie. Using a small spatula, spread mixture nearly to edge. Place a cherry half in the center, if desired.

5. Bake until cookies are golden brown (10 to 12 minutes). Transfer to wire racks to cool.

Makes about forty-two 3-inch cookies.

SWEDISH OATMEAL CRISPS

Scandinavian influence brings elegance to these oatmeal cookies—thanks to a lavish hand with butter and a preference for the subtle flavor of golden raisins over the more common dark variety. The result is a cookie of remarkable style and crispness.

>   1   cup flour
>   1   teaspoon baking soda
>   ½   cup butter or margarine, softened
>   ¾   cup sugar
>   1   egg yolk
>   ½   cup quick-cooking rolled oats
>   ½   cup golden raisins

1. In a bowl stir together flour and baking soda to combine thoroughly; set aside.

2. Preheat oven to 425° F. In mixer bowl combine butter and sugar; beat until fluffy and well blended. Beat in egg yolk.

3. Gradually beat in flour mixture until just blended. Stir in rolled oats and raisins.

4. Shape dough into 1-inch balls. Place about 1½ inches apart on ungreased baking sheets. Press each cookie with tines of a fork to flatten to a thickness of ½ inch.

5. Bake until cookies are golden brown (8 to 10 minutes). Let stand on baking sheets for about 2 minutes, then transfer to wire racks to cool.

Makes about thirty 2½-inch cookies.

CHOCO–PEANUT BUTTER COOKIES

Speckled with grated semisweet chocolate, these peanut butter cookies give a classic recipe new flavor. You can also make these cookies with almond butter, with or without the chocolate.

>   1½ cups flour
>   2   teaspoons baking powder
>   ⅛   teaspoon salt
>   ½   cup butter or margarine, softened
>   ½   cup peanut butter
>   ½   cup each granulated sugar and firmly packed brown sugar
>   1   teaspoon vanilla extract
>   1   egg
>   1   square (1 oz) semisweet baking chocolate, grated

1. In a bowl stir together flour, baking powder, and salt to combine thoroughly; set aside. Preheat oven to 375° F.

2. In mixer bowl combine butter and peanut butter; beat until fluffy. Add sugars and beat until well combined. Blend in vanilla, then egg, and beat until fluffy. Gradually add flour mixture, beating until well blended. Stir in chocolate.

3. Shape dough into 1-inch balls. Place about 1½ inches apart on ungreased baking sheets. Flatten each cookie with a fork, pressing tines once into dough and then crisscrossing the first pattern to make a cross-hatch design.

4. Bake until cookies are lightly browned and feel firm when touched gently (10 to 12 minutes). Transfer to wire racks to cool.

Makes about forty-two 2-inch cookies.

Almond Butter Cookies Substitute almond butter for peanut butter; omit chocolate, if desired.

PECAN POLVORONES

Inspired by a trip in pecan season to the colorful Mexican market town of Ocotlán, these melt-in-the-mouth cookies are a natural to serve with tart lime ice or sliced papaya with a squeeze of lime juice.

>   2¼ cups flour
>   ½   teaspoon ground cinnamon
>   Pinch salt
>   ½   cup butter or margarine, softened
>   ½   cup lard, at room temperature
>   ¾   cup sugar
>   1   egg yolk
>   1   teaspoon vanilla extract
>   ½   cup finely chopped pecans
>   3   tablespoons (approximately) Vanilla Granulated Sugar (see page 39)

1. In a medium-sized bowl stir together flour, cinnamon, and salt to combine thoroughly; set aside. Preheat oven to 350° F.

2. In mixer bowl combine butter and lard; beat until fluffy. Add sugar and beat until well blended. Beat in egg yolk and vanilla. Gradually add flour mixture to butter mixture, beating until well combined. Blend in pecans.

3. Shape dough into 1-inch balls; roll in Vanilla Granulated Sugar to coat generously. Place cookies about 2 inches apart on ungreased baking sheets. Dip a flat-bottomed glass in sugar, and use it to flatten each cookie to a thickness of about ½ inch.

4. Bake for 10 minutes. Reduce heat to 300° F and continue baking until cookies are lightly browned (12 to 15 minutes). Let stand on baking sheets for 1 to 2 minutes, then transfer to wire racks to cool.

Makes about 3 dozen 2½-inch cookies.

TAHINI-GINGER COOKIES

Tahini is a nutlike paste made from ground sesame seed—look for it in stores featuring Middle Eastern foods. Many people liken the texture of tahini to that of peanut butter. These cookies exploit that similarity and complement the exotic flavor of tahini with the sharp sweetness of ginger marmalade.

    1½ cups flour
     2 teaspoons baking powder
     ¼ teaspoon ground cardamom
     ⅛ teaspoon salt
     ½ cup butter or margarine,
        softened
     ½ cup tahini
     ½ cup each granulated
        sugar and firmly packed
        brown sugar
     ½ teaspoon vanilla extract
     1 egg yolk
     ⅔ cup (approximately) ginger
        marmalade or ginger
        preserves

1. In a bowl stir together flour, baking powder, cardamom, and salt to combine thoroughly; set aside. Preheat oven to 375° F.

2. In mixer bowl combine butter and tahini; beat until fluffy. Add sugars and beat until well combined. Blend in vanilla, then egg yolk, beating until fluffy. Gradually add flour mixture, beating until well combined.

3. Shape dough into 1-inch balls. Place about 1½ inches apart on ungreased baking sheets. Slightly flatten each cookie with your fingers. With your finger or teaspoon, make a depression in the center. Bake for 5 minutes. Press depressions down again, then continue baking until cookies are lightly browned and feel firm when touched gently (5 to 7 minutes).

4. Transfer cookies to wire racks to cool. Fill centers with marmalade, dividing it evenly.

Makes about 3 dozen 2½-inch cookies.

NEW MEXICO ANISE COOKIES

The cinnamon and anise flavors in these tender sugar cookies—known to New Mexicans as *biscochitos*—complement foamy hot chocolate on a wintry day.

     3 cups flour
    1½ teaspoons baking powder
     1 teaspoon anise seed, crushed
     ¼ teaspoon salt
     ½ cup butter or margarine,
        softened
     ½ cup lard, at room temperature
     ¾ cup sugar
     1 teaspoon vanilla extract
     1 egg
     2 tablespoons brandy or
        orange juice

Cinnamon Sugar

     ⅓ cup sugar
     1 teaspoon ground cinnamon

1. In a bowl stir together flour, baking powder, anise seed, and salt to combine thoroughly; set aside. Preheat oven to 350° F.

2. In mixer bowl combine butter and lard; beat until fluffy. Add sugar and beat until well combined. Blend in vanilla, then egg. Add flour mixture alternately with brandy, beating until blended after each addition.

3. Shape dough into 1-inch balls. Place about 2 inches apart on lightly greased baking sheets. Dip a flat-bottomed glass in Cinnamon Sugar, and use it to flatten each cookie to a thickness of about ¼ inch. Lightly sprinkle cookies with additional Cinnamon Sugar.

4. Bake until cookies feel firm when touched gently and edges are slightly browned (10 to 12 minutes). Transfer to wire racks to cool.

Makes about 4 dozen 2½-inch cookies.

Cinnamon Sugar In a small bowl mix together sugar and cinnamon.

CRESCENTS AND STRANDS

You can shape these rich, malleable cookie doughs into intriguing forms. Start with a half-moon crescent, then progress to a strand twisted into a pretzel or two strands twined into a plait.

FUDGE MOONS

Chopped hazelnuts or almonds lend chewiness to these appealing chocolate crescents. Serve them with fresh strawberries and whipped cream.

    1¾ cups flour
     ¼ cup unsweetened cocoa
     ½ teaspoon each *baking powder
        and baking soda*
     ¾ cup butter or margarine,
        softened
    1¾ cups confectioners' sugar
     1 teaspoon vanilla extract
     1 egg
     ½ cup chopped unblanched
        hazelnuts or almonds
     2 tablespoons (approximately)
        Vanilla Confectioners' Sugar
        (see page 39)

1. In a bowl stir together flour, cocoa, baking powder, and baking soda to blend thoroughly; set aside. Preheat oven to 350° F.

2. In mixer bowl combine butter and confectioners' sugar; beat until well blended. Mix in vanilla. Add egg and beat until fluffy. Gradually add flour mixture, beating until well combined. Stir in hazelnuts. Gather dough into a ball and enclose in plastic wrap. Refrigerate until firm enough to shape (about 45 minutes).

3. Work with about one fourth of the dough at a time, keeping remainder in refrigerator. Using about 1 tablespoon of dough for each cookie, shape dough into a strand about 3 inches long, then curve into a crescent. Place crescents about 2 inches apart on greased baking sheets.

4. Bake until cookies feel firm when touched gently (12 to 14 minutes). Transfer to wire racks to cool. Lightly sift with Vanilla Confectioners' Sugar.

Makes about 4 dozen cookies.

SPECULAAS—SPICY DUTCH COOKIES

Combining almonds, cinnamon, and other assertive spices is a characteristic of Dutch baking.

DUTCH SPICE COOKIES

These cookies are made authentically by pressing the dough into carved wooden molds. The Dutch name for the cookies, *speculaas*, comes from the Latin word for mirror, *speculum*. It is thought the cookies were so named because they were the mirror image of a mold's design. The carving of speculaas molds is a form of folk art. The wooden plaques contain such deeply incised figures as fanciful birds and beasts, mermaids, ships with billowing sails, and the familiar windmills.

- *¼ cup unblanched almonds*
- *1⅓ cups flour*
- *1½ teaspoons ground cinnamon*
- *½ teaspoon ground cloves*
- *¼ teaspoon each baking powder and ground nutmeg*
  Pinch salt
- *½ cup butter or margarine, softened*
- *⅔ cup firmly packed brown sugar*
- *1 tablespoon rum or apple juice*

1. Place almonds in blender or food processor; whirl or process until powdery.

2. In a bowl stir together ground almonds, flour, cinnamon, cloves, baking powder, nutmeg, and salt to combine thoroughly; set aside.

3. In mixer bowl combine butter and brown sugar, and beat until fluffy and well blended. Gradually beat in half of the flour mixture. Add rum; gradually blend in the remaining flour mixture. Shape dough into a flattened ball.

4. Preheat oven to 325° F. Pinch off 1-inch-diameter balls of dough. Press each firmly and evenly into a floured wooden mold with about 2½-inch-tall figures. Tap mold lightly to remove shaped cookie, easing out with point of a knife if necessary. Arrange cookies about 1 inch apart on ungreased baking sheets.

5. Bake until cookies are lightly browned and feel firm when touched gently (15 to 20 minutes). Let cool slightly on baking sheets; remove to wire racks to complete cooling.

Makes about 3 dozen cookies.

ALMOND-FILLED SPECULAAS

Using the same spicy dough as in Dutch Spice Cookies, you can make cookie logs, known as *gefulde speculaas*, filled with fragrant almond paste. The rolls are baked, then cut into thick slices after cooling.

- *1 recipe Dutch Spice Cookies (see above)*
- *1 package (7 oz) almond paste*
- *1 egg, slightly beaten*
- *24 blanched almond halves*

1. Prepare Dutch Spice Cookies dough through step 3. Enclose dough in waxed paper or plastic wrap and refrigerate until firm (about 1 hour).

2. Place dough between sheets of plastic wrap. Roll out to a 10- by 12-inch rectangle. Divide almond paste in half; on a lightly floured surface, roll each half with your fingertips to form a 12-inch-long strand.

3. Cut rectangle of cookie dough in half to make two 5- by 12-inch rectangles. Place an almond paste rope at 12-inch edge of each. Carefully roll each cookie rectangle tightly around rope of almond paste; press long edge and ends over almond paste to seal. Enclose each roll in plastic wrap and refrigerate until firm (at least 2 hours, or overnight).

4. Preheat oven to 325° F. Carefully transfer filled cookie rolls, seam sides down, to a large, lightly greased baking sheet. Brush lightly with beaten egg; space 12 almond halves evenly down the length of each roll. Bake until surface feels firm when touched gently and almonds are browned (25 to 30 minutes).

5. Cool on baking sheet for 10 minutes, then transfer carefully to a wire rack to cool completely. Cut rolls between almonds to make individual cookie slices.

Makes 2 dozen cookies.

Fancifully shaped Brown-Sugar Twists and honey-glazed Pine-Nut Crescents—from Provence—display the comely effects of an inventive hand.

PINE-NUT CRESCENTS

The French are not content to confine their crescent-shaping talents to the breakfast table. These crescent cookies, *croissants aux pignons*, come from Provence.

> 2 cups flour
> ¼ teaspoon ground nutmeg
> Pinch salt
> ⅔ cup butter or margarine, softened
> ½ cup firmly packed brown sugar
> 2 egg yolks
> 1 tablespoon grated orange rind
> ½ teaspoon vanilla extract
> 2 tablespoons honey
> ¾ cup pine nuts or slivered almonds

1. In a bowl stir together flour, nutmeg, and salt to blend thoroughly; set aside. Preheat oven to 350° F.

2. In mixer bowl combine butter and brown sugar; beat until fluffy. Add egg yolks, one at a time, beating well after each addition. Blend in orange rind and vanilla. Gradually add flour mixture, beating until thoroughly combined.

3. Using about 1 tablespoon of dough for each cookie, shape dough into a strand about 3 inches long, then curve into a crescent. Place crescents about 2 inches apart on greased baking sheets.

4. Heat honey in a small pan over low heat until fluid and just warm to the touch. Lightly brush honey over tops and sides of crescents, then liberally coat with pine nuts, pressing them in gently.

5. Bake until cookies are golden (10 to 12 minutes). Let cool on baking sheets for 1 to 2 minutes, then transfer to wire racks to complete cooling.

Makes about 30 cookies.

FRUITED WALNUT RINGS

These ring-shaped variations of Pine-Nut Crescents with candied fruit—called *gimblettes d'Albi*—originated in Albi, in southwestern France.

> 2 cups flour
> ¼ teaspoon ground nutmeg
> Pinch salt
> ⅔ cup butter or margarine, softened
> ½ cup firmly packed brown sugar
> 2 egg yolks (reserve 1 white for coating)
> 1 tablespoon grated orange rind
> ½ teaspoon vanilla extract
> ½ cup finely chopped walnuts
> ¼ cup very finely chopped citron, angelica, or candied pineapple
> 1 tablespoon honey

1. In a bowl stir together flour, nutmeg, and salt to blend thoroughly; set aside. Preheat oven to 350° F.

2. In a mixer bowl combine butter and brown sugar; beat until fluffy. Add egg yolks, one at a time, beating well after each addition. Blend in orange rind and vanilla. Gradually add flour mixture, beating until well combined. Stir in walnuts and citron.

3. Using about 1 tablespoon of dough for each cookie, shape dough into a strand 4 inches long. Form each strand into a ring, pinching ends to seal. Place rings about 2 inches apart on well-greased baking sheets.

4. In a small bowl beat egg white with honey until frothy. Brush mixture on cookies.

5. Bake until golden (10 to 12 minutes). Let cool on baking sheets for 1 to 2 minutes, then transfer to wire racks to complete cooling.

Makes 3 dozen cookies.

BROWN-SUGAR TWISTS

A buttery brown-sugar dough is twisted into fancy cookie sticks. Sprinkled with sugar and almonds, these have a rich crispness that is hard to resist.

> 1½ cups flour
> ½ teaspoon ground cinnamon
> ⅛ teaspoon salt
> ⅔ cup butter or margarine, softened
> ½ cup firmly packed brown sugar
> 2 tablespoons coffee liqueur or coffee brandy
> 2 tablespoons each ground unblanched almonds and granulated sugar

1. In a bowl stir together flour, cinnamon, and salt to combine thoroughly; set aside.

2. In a mixer bowl combine butter and brown sugar; beat until fluffy. Blend in coffee liqueur. Gradually add flour mixture, beating just until smoothly blended. Gather dough into a ball and enclose in plastic wrap. Refrigerate until firm enough to shape (about 45 minutes).

3. Preheat oven to 375° F. Work with about one fourth of the dough at a time, keeping remainder in refrigerator. Using about 1 tablespoon dough for each cookie, shape dough into a strand 8 inches long; cut strand into two 4-inch-long pieces. Carefully twist the 2 strands together. Place cookies about 1½ inches apart on lightly greased baking sheets.

4. In a small bowl stir together almonds and granulated sugar. Sprinkle mixture over cookies.

5. Bake until lightly browned and firm when touched gently (10 to 12 minutes). Let stand on baking sheets for about 2 minutes, then transfer to wire racks to cool completely.

Makes about 3 dozen cookies.

CHOCOLATE PRETZELS

These trompe l'oeil pretzels speckled with coarse sugar are as appropriate with a demitasse of strong coffee as are their salty counterparts with a stein of beer.

- 1⅔ cups flour
- ¼ cup unsweetened cocoa
- ¾ cup butter or margarine, softened
- ¾ cup granulated sugar
- 1 teaspoon vanilla extract
- 1 egg white, slightly beaten
- 2 tablespoons coarse sugar (pearl or decorating sugar, or crushed sugar cubes)

1. In a bowl stir together flour and cocoa to combine well; set aside.

2. In mixer bowl combine butter and granulated sugar; beat until fluffy. Blend in vanilla. Gradually add flour mixture, beating until smooth. Gather dough into a ball and enclose in plastic wrap. Refrigerate until firm enough to shape (about 45 minutes).

3. Preheat oven to 350° F. Work with one fourth of the dough at a time, keeping remainder in refrigerator. Divide each portion into 8 equal pieces. On a lightly floured pastry cloth or board, roll each piece into an 8-inch-long strand using the palms of your hands. Twist each strand into pretzel shape. Place cookies about 1 inch apart on lightly greased baking sheets.

4. Lightly brush each cookie with beaten egg white, then scatter coarse sugar over surface.

5. Bake until cookies feel firm when touched lightly (12 to 14 minutes). Let stand on baking sheets for about 2 minutes, then transfer to wire racks to cool completely.

Makes 32 cookies.

ALMOND-BUTTER CRESCENTS

If your grandmother came from Greece, you may know these irresistible, powdered sugar–smothered cookies as *kourabiedes*. If she hailed from Austria, you may know them as *Kipfels*. It's hard to find a more appealing cookie in any language.

- 2½ cups flour
- ¼ teaspoon salt
- ½ cup very finely chopped or ground unblanched almonds
- 1 cup butter or margarine, softened
- ½ cup granulated sugar
- 1 egg yolk
- 1 teaspoon brandy or lemon juice
- 1½ cups (approximately) Vanilla Confectioners' Sugar (see page 39)

1. In a bowl stir together flour, salt, and almonds to combine thoroughly; set aside. Preheat oven to 350° F.

2. In mixer bowl combine butter and granulated sugar; beat until fluffy. Blend in egg yolk, then brandy. Gradually add flour mixture, beating just until dough clings together.

3. Using about 1 tablespoon of dough for each cookie, shape dough into a strand about 3 inches long, then curve into a crescent. Place crescents about 1½ inches apart on ungreased baking sheets.

4. Bake until cookies are lightly browned and feel firm when touched gently (15 to 18 minutes).

5. Spread about ¾ cup of the Vanilla Confectioners' Sugar on a rimmed baking sheet. As cookies finish baking, remove them to sugar-lined baking sheet. Generously sift some of the remaining Vanilla Confectioners' Sugar over warm cookies, turning them in sugar if necessary to coat all surfaces liberally. Transfer to wire racks to complete cooling.

Makes about 42 cookies.

COOKIE TARTS

Cookie dough pressed into diminutive muffin pans makes bite-sized cookie tarts suitable for important occasions. With buttery-rich pastry and intensely flavored nut, lemon, or chocolate fillings, these are the sort of delicacies the French serve with coffee after an elegant dinner.

GLAZED ALMOND TARTS

The almonds in the tender pastry of these currant jelly–glazed morsels echo the almond paste in the filling.

- ½ cup prepared almond paste
- ¼ cup butter or margarine, softened
- 1 egg white
- ¼ cup confectioners' sugar
- 1 tablespoon orange flower water
- ⅓ cup red currant or raspberry jelly

Press-In Pastry

- 1 cup flour
- 2 tablespoons ground unblanched almonds
- 3 tablespoons Vanilla Confectioners' Sugar (see page 39)
- ⅓ cup firm butter or margarine
- 1 egg yolk
- 2 teaspoons water

1. Pinch off ¾-inch balls of Press-In Pastry and press into ungreased 1¾-inch muffin pans. Preheat oven to 350° F.

2. In a mixer bowl combine almond paste, butter, egg white, confectioners' sugar, and orange flower water; beat until fluffy and well blended. Fill each pastry shell about two thirds full with almond-paste mixture.

3. Bake until pastry is browned and filling is set (25 to 30 minutes). Let tarts cool in pans on wire racks.

4. Heat jelly in a small pan over medium heat, stirring until jelly bubbles and melts. Spoon a little melted jelly over each tart. When tarts are cool, remove from pans.

Makes 2 dozen cookies.

Press-In Pastry In a bowl stir together flour, ground almonds, and Vanilla Confectioners' Sugar to combine thoroughly. Using a pastry blender or 2 knives, cut in butter until mixture resembles coarse crumbs. In a small bowl combine egg yolk and the water; beat until blended. Add egg mixture to flour mixture, stirring with a fork until dough clings together. Use your hands to press dough into a smooth ball.

BITE-SIZED LEMON TARTS

Homemade lemon curd is the filling for these sunny cookies, which are made with an easily handled cream-cheese pastry.

¼ cup butter or margarine
1 teaspoon grated lemon rind
¼ cup lemon juice
⅔ cup granulated sugar
2 eggs

Cream-Cheese Pastry

½ cup butter or margarine, softened
1 small package (3 oz) cream cheese, softened
2 tablespoons confectioners' sugar
1 tablespoon brandy
1¼ cups flour

1. In top of a double boiler melt butter over direct low heat. Remove from heat and add lemon rind, lemon juice, granulated sugar, and eggs. Beat with whisk until well combined.

2. Place lemon mixture over simmering water and cook, stirring often, until thickened and smooth (about 10 to 15 minutes). Remove top of double boiler to a wire rack and let filling cool until it is barely warm to the touch.

3. Preheat oven to 350° F. Divide Cream-Cheese Pastry evenly in ungreased 1¾-inch muffin pans, using your fingertips to press pastry uniformly into each cup. Pierce each pastry shell in several places with a fork.

4. Bake until pastry shells are golden brown (18 to 20 minutes). Cool in pans on wire racks.

5. Fill pastry shells with lemon filling. Remove tarts from pans and serve either at room temperature or chilled.

Makes 2 dozen cookies.

Cream-Cheese Pastry In a mixer bowl combine butter, cream cheese, and confectioners' sugar; beat until light and fluffy. Blend in brandy. Gradually add flour, mixing until dough is smooth.

Tips

MAKING AN IMPRESSION WITH COOKIE STAMPS

As you browse through mail-order cookware catalogs, well-stocked housewares stores, or even a crafts fair, you may come upon intriguing cookie stamps.

Fashioned from glass or ceramic, the stamps have a deep intaglio design that can be transferred to cookie dough, which retains the pattern during baking.

To make cookies with such stamps, choose a molded cookie dough that will take impressions well—a dough that's firm and not so buttery rich that the designs will melt away as the cookies bake.

If you have a favorite recipe for cookies that are shaped by being pressed, one at a time, into an unglazed stoneware mold, such a dough will also retain the impression of a cookie stamp.

Other good choices include Browned Butter Balls (see page 58) and Pine-Nut Crescents (see page 69; do not brush cookies with honey or coat with pine nuts).

Shape the dough into 1-inch balls (or larger, if the cookie stamp exceeds 2 inches in diameter). Place the balls of dough on a baking sheet and use the cookie stamp to press each ball of dough into an evenly flattened round the same size as the stamp. If necessary, dust the stamp with flour or dip it into granulated sugar between each use to prevent the dough from sticking to it.

Bake the cookies as directed in the recipe, checking for doneness 2 to 3 minutes before the time specified in the recipe. (Because the stamped cookies are thinner, they may bake faster.)

Cocoa Pastry

- 1 cup flour
- 1 tablespoon unsweetened cocoa
- 3 tablespoons Vanilla Confectioners' Sugar (see page 39)
- ⅓ cup firm butter or margarine
- 1 egg yolk
- 2 teaspoons water

1. Preheat oven to 350° F. Pinch off 1-inch balls of Cocoa Pastry and press into ungreased 1¾-inch muffin pans. Bake until lightly browned and firm when touched gently (10 to 15 minutes).

2. Let tart shells cool in pans on wire racks. Carefully remove shells from muffin pans. Spoon a scant ½ teaspoon raspberry jam into each.

3. In a heavy pan over low heat, combine chocolate, Vanilla Granulated Sugar, and butter. Heat, stirring occasionally, until chocolate and butter melt and sugar is dissolved. Add whipping cream; stir over medium heat until mixture is hot to the touch (2 to 3 minutes). Remove from heat and let stand until cooled to room temperature (about 20 minutes).

4. Spoon about ½ tablespoon of the chocolate filling into each tart shell. Let stand at room temperature until filling is set (about 1 hour).

Makes 2 dozen cookies.

Cocoa Pastry In a bowl stir together flour, cocoa, and Vanilla Confectioners' Sugar to combine thoroughly. Using a pastry blender or 2 knives, cut in butter until mixture resembles coarse crumbs. In a small bowl combine egg yolk and the water; beat until blended. Add egg mixture to flour mixture, stirring with a fork until dough clings together. Use your hands to press dough into a smooth ball.

Chocolate-Filled Chocolate Nests are cookies with the appeal of a chocolate truffle. They make a dainty treat with an after-dinner demitasse. For a glamorous garnish, pipe on a whipped cream kiss and top with a fresh raspberry.

CHOCOLATE-FILLED CHOCOLATE NESTS

A creamy chocolate filling conceals a raspberry layer atop the crisp cocoa press-in pastry.

- ¼ cup raspberry jam or preserves
- 4 ounces semisweet chocolate, coarsely chopped
- 2 tablespoons Vanilla Granulated Sugar (see page 39)
- 2 tablespoons butter or margarine
- ¼ cup whipping cream

DELICATE, SHELL-SHAPED MADELEINES

Even people who haven't studied French literature might be aware that the delicate cookie the French call a *madeleine* is the inspiration for Marcel Proust's evocative novel *Remembrance of Things Past*. You don't have to be an accomplished baker to recognize a madeleine pan, with its rows of shell-shaped impressions.

These cookies are perhaps too subtle for the reputation that precedes them. Their gentle flavor is derived from browned butter. The texture of these classic cookies is similar to that of a sponge cake.

Traditionally, madeleines are baked in a gleaming tin plaque. Pans with a nonstick coating are now available; with very little greasing they turn out perfect cookies easily.

½ cup unsalted butter
2 eggs
½ cup sugar
1 teaspoon finely grated lemon rind
¼ teaspoon lemon juice
¼ teaspoon vanilla extract
⅛ teaspoon baking powder
¾ cup sifted cake flour

1. In a saucepan over medium heat, melt butter until the milk solids turn a golden brown color. (This will occur just after the foam subsides.) Transfer to a small stainless steel bowl and allow to cool for 10 minutes.

2. In a medium stainless steel bowl over boiling water, whisk eggs and sugar until mixture is tepid (98° F). Remove from heat and whisk in lemon rind, lemon juice, and vanilla. Sift baking powder and flour together; stir into egg mixture. Stir in melted and cooled butter. Cover bowl with plastic wrap and allow to rest for 1 hour at room temperature.

3. Preheat oven to 450° F. Brush insides of shells of madeleine pans with a thin layer of melted butter. Dust with flour, then invert pan and rap briskly on counter to remove excess flour. Spoon batter into shells, filling each three fourths full.

4. Bake until cookies rise in center and are very light brown on the bottom and edges (3 to 4 minutes for 1½-inch madeleines, 10 to 12 minutes for 3-inch madeleines). When done they spring back when lightly touched in the center. Remove madeleines from oven, invert pan over wire cooling rack, and tap lightly to release cookies from pan.

5. Cookies are best when served while still warm. Otherwise, cool completely and store in an airtight container or freeze until ready to use.

Makes 40 small or 15 large madeleines.

HOW TO SHAPE FORTUNE COOKIES

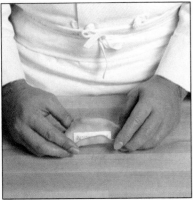

1. *Holding hot cookie flat, place fortune strip in center. Gently fold cookie in half. (If you find cookies too hot to handle, wear gloves.)*

2. *Crease folded cookie by drawing its center across edge of bowl.*

3. *Ensure softly rounded shape of cookies by placing them, pointed ends down, in muffin pans until cool and firm.*

FORTUNE COOKIES

Fortune cookies are first baked, then molded, into their distinctive form. A strip of paper bearing a tersely stated fortune is inserted; then the hot-from-the-oven cookie is folded to enclose it.

Although a meal in a Chinese restaurant wouldn't be complete without fortune cookies, it's doubtful that they are actually Chinese. However, they're one of the pleasures of Chinese-American dining. The next time you plan a dinner of Chinese food, serve these with tea for dessert. You'll find they taste better than most, because they are flavored with orange flower water and orange rind.

You should bake only 2 or 3 cookies at a time so you can fold them all before they become too stiff. If the last cookie in a batch does firm up, you can restore its flexibility by returning it to the oven for 10 to 20 seconds.

As soon as the cookies cool, they become brittle and crisp. It's important to work with the cookies the instant you remove them from the oven. Wearing soft, snug-fitting, cotton gloves will help you to handle the hot cookies without discomfort.

> ½ cup flour
> 1 tablespoon cornstarch
> ¼ cup sugar
> ¼ cup salad oil (such as corn or safflower)
> 2 egg whites (about ¼ cup)
> 1 tablespoon orange flower water
> ½ teaspoon grated orange rind
> 12 to 16 fortunes, typed on ½- by 3-inch strips of paper (see Note)

1. In mixer bowl stir together flour, cornstarch, and sugar to combine thoroughly.

2. Preheat oven to 325° F. To flour mixture add oil and egg whites; beat at high speed until smooth. Mix in orange flower water and orange rind.

3. Make just 2 or 3 cookies at a time, dropping batter by level tablespoons, placed about 3 inches apart, onto a well-greased baking sheet. Use a small spatula or the back of a spoon to spread each portion of batter evenly to a 4-inch-diameter circle.

4. Bake until cookies are a light golden brown (10 to 12 minutes).

5. Using a wide, flexible spatula, immediately remove 1 hot cookie at a time from baking sheet. Holding cookie flat with smooth side (which was against baking sheet) down, place fortune in center. Then quickly make the following folds pictured in photographs at left.

6. Gently fold cookie in half to make half-moon shape, with curved (open) side facing upward.

7. Create second fold by drawing center of folded cookie (open edges up) across a thin-edged bowl or pan to crease cookie in half again.

8. To preserve typical fortune-cookie shape, place each folded cookie, pointed ends down, in cup of muffin pan until cookies are completely cooled and feel firm to the touch.

9. Using remaining batter, repeat steps 3 through 8 until all cookies are baked, shaped, and cooled. Store cookies in tightly covered metal container or sealed plastic bag for up to a week.

Makes 12 to 16 cookies.

<u>Note</u> Consult an Asian fortune-telling book for appropriate messages, or look at a book of quotations for appropriate witticisms and maxims.

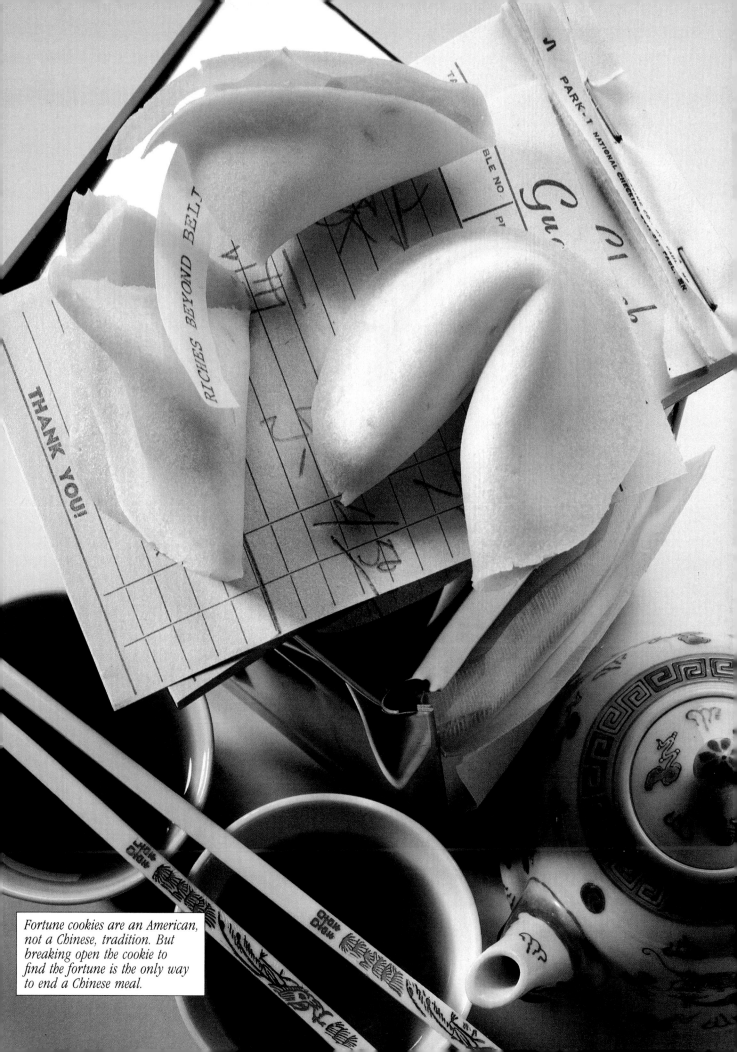

Fortune cookies are an American, not a Chinese, tradition. But breaking open the cookie to find the fortune is the only way to end a Chinese meal.

Chocolate sprinkles speckle these easy-to-make refrigerator cookies. The recipe for crisp, rich Chocolate Tweed Cookies is on page 85.

Refrigerator Cookies

Long before there were cookie mixes or plastic-encased rolls of cookie dough in the supermarket refrigerator case, there were "icebox cookies"—one of the original convenience foods. These homemade cookies were created from dough that had been lovingly enclosed in waxed paper and set aside to chill and be baked later. Today many kinds of cookies benefit from spending some time in the refrigerator—or freezer—before baking (see page 83).

Your food processor makes light work of any one of these three refrigerator cookies, provocatively flavored with (clockwise from left) orange and hazelnuts, ginger and walnuts, and coffee and pecans.

HANDY, BAKE-ANYTIME COOKIES

Being able to mix now and bake later makes refrigerator cookies a favorite with busy people. The rich dough for these cookies can be made quickly and stored for up to 3 days in the refrigerator for future pleasure. Then you can bake the entire batch or as many cookies as you want.

Because refrigerator cookies are sliced thinly from a roll of dough, solid ingredients must be either finely chopped or pliable enough so the dough can be sliced easily without tearing.

THREE-WAY FOOD-PROCESSOR COOKIE SLICES

The food processor does most of the work involved in producing this cookie dough, from chopping the nuts to combining all the ingredients into an easy-to-shape ball. The three enticing combinations of flavors are orange with hazelnuts, coffee with pecans, and ginger with walnuts.

- ½ cup unblanched hazelnuts
- 1 cup sugar
- 2 tablespoons grated orange rind
- ½ cup plus 2 tablespoons firm butter, diced
- 1 tablespoon lemon juice
- 1 egg yolk
- 1½ cups flour

1. In work bowl of food processor, combine nuts, sugar, and orange rind; process until nuts are finely chopped.

2. Add butter and process, using short on-off bursts, until butter is evenly incorporated into nut mixture. Add lemon juice and egg yolk; process until well blended.

3. With motor running, gradually add flour through feed tube, processing just until all flour is incorporated and mixture begins to form a ball.

4. Divide dough in half, transfer each half to a sheet of waxed paper or plastic wrap. Using a spatula and the paper, shape each half into a 2-inch-diameter log. Wrap each log tightly. Refrigerate until firm—at least 2 hours, or overnight (or place in freezer for 30 to 45 minutes).

5. Preheat oven to 375° F. Cut logs into ¼-inch-thick slices; arrange slices, about 1 inch apart, on lightly greased baking sheets.

6. Bake until edges of cookies are golden brown (10 to 12 minutes). Transfer to wire racks to cool.

Makes about 4 dozen 2½-inch cookies.

Coffee-Pecan Slices Omit hazelnuts; substitute ½ cup pecans. Use ½ cup each granulated sugar and firmly packed brown sugar in place of the 1 cup sugar. Add ¾ teaspoon powdered or granulated instant coffee with nuts and sugar. Omit orange rind. Omit lemon juice; substitute 1 tablespoon coffee-flavored liqueur.

Ginger Slices Omit hazelnuts; substitute ⅓ cup walnuts. Add ½ teaspoon ground ginger and 1 tablespoon coarsely chopped crystallized ginger with nuts and sugar. Omit orange rind. Omit lemon juice; substitute 1 tablespoon rum.

JAN HAGEL COOKIES

The pungent flavors of cinnamon and almonds permeate every crumb of these typically Dutch cookies. They are named for the innovative nineteenth-century baker who perfected them.

>   1½ *cups flour*
>   1 *teaspoon ground cinnamon*
>   ½ *cup firmly packed brown sugar*
>   ½ *cup sliced almonds*
>   ¾ *cup firm butter or margarine, diced*
>   ½ *teaspoon vanilla extract*
>   *Vanilla Granulated Sugar (see page 39)*

1. In a large bowl stir together flour, cinnamon, brown sugar, and almonds to combine thoroughly.

2. Using a pastry blender or 2 knives, cut in butter until all particles are uniformly small and well coated with flour mixture. Stir in vanilla. Use your hands to press dough firmly into a smooth ball.

3. Divide dough in half; transfer each half to a sheet of waxed paper or plastic wrap. Shape each half into a 2-inch-diameter log. Wrap each log tightly. Refrigerate until firm—at least 2 hours, or overnight (or place in freezer for 30 to 45 minutes).

4. Preheat oven to 400° F. Cut logs into ¼-inch-thick slices; arrange slices, about 1 inch apart, on greased baking sheets. Sprinkle lightly with Vanilla Granulated Sugar. Bake until cookies are lightly browned and feel firm when touched gently (8 to 10 minutes). Transfer cookies to wire racks to cool.

Makes about forty-two 2½-inch cookies.

COCOA–PEANUT BUTTER COOKIES

Crisp, rich, and decidedly peanut butter-flavored, these fudgelike cookies are the ultimate snack with a glass of cold milk.

>   ⅔ *cup flour*
>   ½ *cup unsweetened cocoa*
>   ¾ *teaspoon baking powder*
>   ¼ *teaspoon baking soda*
>   ½ *cup butter or margarine, softened*
>   ⅓ *cup peanut butter*
>   ⅔ *cup sugar*
>   1 *egg*
>   ½ *cup chocolate sprinkles*

1. In a medium bowl stir together flour, cocoa, baking powder, and baking soda to combine thoroughly; set aside.

2. In mixer bowl combine butter and peanut butter; beat to blend thoroughly. Add sugar and beat until fluffy. Beat in egg.

3. Gradually add flour mixture, beating until just blended. Stir in chocolate sprinkles.

4. Divide dough in half; transfer each half to a sheet of waxed paper or plastic wrap. Using a spatula and the paper, shape each half into a 2-inch-diameter log. Wrap each log tightly. Refrigerate until firm—at least 2 hours, or overnight (or place in freezer for 30 to 45 minutes).

5. Preheat oven to 350° F. Cut logs into ¼-inch-thick slices; arrange slices, about 1 inch apart, on ungreased baking sheets. Bake until cookies are just firm to the touch (10 to 12 minutes). Let stand for about 2 minutes, then transfer to wire racks to cool.

Makes about forty-two 2½-inch cookies.

BRETON HAZELNUT CRISPS

Brushing these nut-studded slices with egg white and sprinkling them with sugar before baking adds a sparkling finish.

 1¼ cups flour
  1 teaspoon cream of tartar
  ½ teaspoon baking soda
  ¼ teaspoon salt
  ½ cup butter or margarine, softened
  ¼ cup granulated sugar
  ½ cup firmly packed brown sugar
  1 teaspoon vanilla extract
  2 eggs, separated
  2 tablespoons milk
  1 cup coarsely chopped unblanched hazelnuts
    Vanilla Granulated Sugar (see page 39)

1. In a bowl stir together flour, cream of tartar, baking soda, and salt to combine thoroughly; set aside.

2. In mixer bowl combine butter and sugars; beat until fluffy and well blended, then beat in vanilla. Add egg yolks, one at a time, beating well after each addition.

3. Add flour mixture alternately with milk, blending well after each addition. Stir in hazelnuts.

4. Divide dough in half; transfer each half to a sheet of waxed paper or plastic wrap. Using a spatula and the paper, shape each half into a 2-inch-diameter log, then flatten each slightly. Wrap each log tightly. Refrigerate until firm—at least 2 hours, or overnight (or place in freezer for 30 to 45 minutes).

5. Preheat oven to 375° F. Cut logs into ¼-inch-thick slices; arrange slices, 2 inches apart, on greased baking sheets.

6. In a small bowl beat egg whites with 1½ teaspoons water. Brush cookies with egg-white mixture, then sprinkle lightly with Vanilla Granulated Sugar.

7. Bake until cookies are golden brown (10 to 12 minutes). Let cool for about 2 minutes on baking sheets, then remove to wire racks to cool completely.

Makes about forty-two 3-inch cookies.

BUTTERY PECAN SLICES

Pecans coat the outer surfaces and permeate the interior of these buttery cookies, promising an abundance of toasted nut flavor and crispness in every bite.

  1 cup butter or margarine, softened
  1 cup confectioners' sugar
 1½ teaspoons vanilla extract
 1½ cups flour
  2 cups finely chopped pecans

1. In mixer bowl beat butter and sugar until fluffy; beat in vanilla.

2. Gradually add flour, mixing until well combined. Add 1 cup of the pecans; stir to blend.

3. Spread ½ cup of the remaining pecans on a sheet of waxed paper or plastic wrap.

4. Divide dough in half; transfer half to nut-coated paper. Using a spatula and the paper, shape dough into a 1½-inch-diameter log, coating all sides evenly with nuts. Repeat with remaining pecans and other half of cookie dough. Wrap each log tightly in waxed paper or plastic wrap. Refrigerate until firm—at least 2 hours, or overnight (or place in freezer for 30 to 45 minutes).

5. Preheat oven to 350° F. Cut logs into ¼-inch-thick slices; place slices, slightly apart, on ungreased baking sheets. Bake until lightly browned (10 to 12 minutes). Let stand on baking sheets for 1 to 3 minutes, then transfer to wire racks to cool.

Makes about 6 dozen 2½-inch cookies.

SPICY RAISIN-OATMEAL ROUNDS

Crisp, spicy, and chewy, these convenient refrigerator-style oatmeal cookies are every bit as irresistible as the drop-cookie version.

  1 cup flour
  ½ teaspoon each baking powder and ground cinnamon
  ¼ teaspoon baking soda
  ⅛ teaspoon salt
  ½ cup butter or margarine, softened
  ⅔ cup sugar
  ½ teaspoon vanilla extract
  1 egg
  ¾ cup quick-cooking rolled oats
  1 cup raisins
  ½ cup finely chopped walnuts

1. In a bowl stir together flour, baking powder, cinnamon, baking soda, and salt to combine thoroughly; set aside.

2. In mixer bowl beat butter and sugar until well combined; blend in vanilla. Add egg and beat until fluffy.

3. Gradually blend in flour mixture until well combined. Stir in rolled oats, raisins, and walnuts.

4. Divide dough in half; transfer each half to a sheet of waxed paper or plastic wrap. Using a spatula and the paper, shape each half into a 2-inch-diameter log. Wrap each log tightly. Refrigerate until firm—at least 2 hours, or overnight (or place in freezer for 30 to 45 minutes).

5. Preheat oven to 375° F. Cut logs into ¼-inch-thick slices; arrange slices, slightly apart, on lightly greased baking sheets. Bake until cookies are golden (8 to 10 minutes). Transfer to wire racks to cool.

Makes about 4 dozen 2-inch cookies.

You'll hear echoes of Brittany in the buttery crunch of Breton Hazelnut Crisps. Serve these nut-encrusted cookies with chilled French hard cider.

Subtly flavored Molasses Crisps are sure to be a welcome addition to the noon fare of the brown bag- and lunch box-toting set.

PINA-COLADA CRISPS

Similar in texture to shortbread—but with the ease and convenience of refrigerator cookies—these crisp wafers are perfect with a tropical-tasting fruit sherbet on a sultry evening. Be sure you use natural-colored candied pineapple, not the red and green kind that is sold at Christmas for fruitcakes.

   1 cup butter or margarine,
      softened
   ½ cup granulated sugar
   ⅛ teaspoon salt
   1 teaspoon vanilla extract
   2 cups flour
   ½ cup finely chopped candied
      pineapple
   1½ cups flaked coconut
   ½ to ¾ cup Vanilla Confection-
      ers' Sugar (see page 39)

1. In mixer bowl beat butter and granulated sugar until fluffy; beat in salt and vanilla.

2. Gradually add flour, mixing until well combined. Stir in pineapple and coconut.

3. Transfer dough to a sheet of waxed paper or plastic wrap; shape into two 1½-inch-diameter logs. Enclose each log in plastic wrap or waxed paper and refrigerate until firm—at least 2 hours, or overnight (or place in freezer for 30 to 45 minutes).

4. Preheat oven to 325° F. Cut dough into ¼-inch-thick slices; arrange slices, slightly apart, on lightly greased baking sheets.

5. Bake cookies until lightly browned (15 to 20 minutes). Transfer to wire racks. While cookies are warm, sift generously with Vanilla Confectioners' Sugar.

Makes about 5 dozen 2-inch cookies.

MOLASSES CRISPS

The molasses flavor of these thin, tender cookies is so subtle that you may need to taste them twice to detect it. They are so delicious that you probably cannot stop at just two.

   1½ cups flour
   1 teaspoon baking soda
   ½ cup butter or margarine,
      softened
   ½ cup vegetable shortening
   ¾ cup sugar
   ½ teaspoon vanilla extract
   ¼ cup light molasses
   1 cup finely chopped walnuts

1. In a bowl stir together flour and baking soda to combine thoroughly; set aside.

2. In mixer bowl beat butter, shortening, and sugar until well combined; blend in vanilla and beat until fluffy.

3. Add flour mixture alternately with molasses, mixing to blend after each addition. Stir in walnuts.

4. Divide dough in half; transfer each half to a sheet of waxed paper or plastic wrap. Shape each half into a 2-inch-diameter log and wrap tightly. Refrigerate until firm—at least 2 hours, or overnight (or place in freezer for 30 to 45 minutes).

5. Preheat oven to 350° F. Carefully cut logs into ¼-inch-thick slices; arrange slices, about 1½ inches apart, on lightly greased baking sheets. Bake until cookies are golden brown (10 to 12 minutes). Let stand on baking sheets for about 2 minutes, then transfer to wire racks to cool.

Makes about sixty-six 2½-inch cookies.

Tips

COOL IDEAS FOR EASIER REFRIGERATOR COOKIES

If making refrigerator cookies is unfamiliar to you, some helpful hints may be in order.

□ Shape dough before chilling it. After beating in dry ingredients and other added elements, dough will be quite soft and creamy. Divide it roughly in half, then turn out each half onto a square of plastic wrap or waxed paper. Using 2 spatulas—and the wrap as a guide—coax dough into a long, fat, sausagelike shape. While lifting and rolling, enclose dough in the wrapping. When dough is confined, you will be able to use your hands to mold it into an even more regular shape.

□ Place wrapped dough in coldest part of refrigerator (or in freezer—but keep track of the time, because it will begin to freeze after about 45 minutes). If dough is very soft and you want to keep the round shape, remove dough and smooth its contours once or twice during the chilling period.

□ To freeze dough for longer storage, enclose it in a moisture-proof wrapping such as freezer wrap or heavy aluminum foil. (Cookies enclosed in waxed paper or plastic wrap should be overwrapped in a sturdier material if you decide to freeze part of the unbaked dough.) Well-wrapped cookie dough can be kept frozen for up to a month.

□ To thaw frozen cookie dough, transfer it from freezer to refrigerator 1 to 2 hours before you plan to slice and bake it. Swirled cookies containing a filling may take a little longer to thaw because the filling becomes much harder when frozen than does the surrounding dough.

REFRIGERATOR COOKIES IN PATTERNS

A well-chilled refrigerator cookie dough is sturdy enough to be a good medium for invention. Taking advantage of contrasting colors and flavors of two refrigerator doughs, you can make the intriguing cookies shown on page 87. Although they take an extra step or two to prepare, these cookies are as convenient to make ahead as less fancy refrigerator cookies.

MULTICOLORED REFRIGERATOR COOKIES

With these illustrations as your guide, you can combine tender, crisp chocolate and butterscotch doughs to make checkerboards, pinwheels, or mosaic refrigerator cookies.

Light Dough

- 1⅓ cups flour
- ½ teaspoon baking powder
- ¼ teaspoon salt
- ½ cup butter or margarine, softened
- ¼ cup vegetable shortening
- ½ cup each granulated sugar and firmly packed brown sugar
- ½ teaspoon vanilla extract
- 1 egg yolk

Chocolate Dough

- 1 cup flour
- ¼ cup unsweetened cocoa
- ½ teaspoon baking soda
- ¼ teaspoon salt
- ½ cup butter or margarine, softened
- ¼ cup vegetable shortening
- ½ cup each granulated sugar and firmly packed brown sugar
- 1 egg

Light Dough

1. In a bowl stir together flour, baking powder, and salt to combine thoroughly; set aside.

2. In mixer bowl combine butter and shortening; beat to blend well. Add sugars and beat until fluffy. Beat in vanilla, then egg yolk.

3. Gradually add flour mixture, beating until just blended. Chill and shape dough as directed for the cookie style of your choice.

Chocolate Dough

1. In a bowl stir together flour, cocoa, baking soda, and salt to combine thoroughly; set aside.

2. In mixer bowl combine butter and shortening; beat to blend well. Add sugars and beat until fluffy. Add egg and beat until well blended.

3. Gradually add flour mixture, beating until just blended. Chill and shape dough as directed for the cookie style of your choice.

To Make Checkerboards

1. Transfer Light Dough to a large sheet of plastic wrap or waxed paper. Using a spatula and the plastic wrap, shape dough into a 2-inch-square log about 9 inches long. Wrap tightly and refrigerate until firm (at least 2 hours, or overnight; or place in freezer for 30 to 45 minutes).

2. Repeat procedure described in step 1 using Chocolate Dough.

3. To make long strips, slice Light Dough lengthwise into halves or thirds. Separate layers and slice each

lengthwise into halves or thirds. You will have 4 strips if you cut dough into halves or 9 strips if you cut dough into thirds.

4. Repeat procedure described in step 3 using Chocolate Dough.

5. Following the illustration, place strips of Light Dough and Chocolate Dough side by side to form 2 logs, alternating colors to make each layer. Wrap each log tightly in plastic wrap, firmly pressing multicolored strips together. Return to refrigerator for at least 3 hours, or overnight.

6. Preheat oven to 350° F. Remove one roll of cookie dough at a time from refrigerator. Slice cookies to a thickness of ¼ inch, and arrange slices about 1 inch apart on ungreased baking sheets.

7. Bake until cookies feel firm when touched lightly (8 to 10 minutes). Transfer to wire racks to cool.

Makes about 6 dozen 2½-inch cookies.

To Make Pinwheels

1. Transfer Light Dough to a large sheet of plastic wrap or waxed paper. Using a spatula, flatten dough into a rectangle about 1 inch thick. Wrap tightly and refrigerate until firm (at least 2 hours, or overnight; or place in freezer for 30 to 45 minutes).

2. Repeat procedure described in step 1 using Chocolate Dough.

3. Place Light Dough between 2 sheets of plastic wrap; roll into a 12-inch by 16-inch rectangle. Remove top sheet of plastic.

4. Repeat procedure described in step 3 using Chocolate Dough.

5. Invert Chocolate Dough over Light Dough; peel off top sheet of plastic wrap. Starting with a 16-inch edge, and using bottom sheet of plastic and a spatula to guide dough, tightly roll 2 sheets of dough together, jelly-roll fashion. Cut roll in half to make two 8-inch-long rolls. Enclose each tightly in plastic wrap; refrigerate for at least 3 hours, or overnight.

6. Preheat oven to 350° F. Slice and bake as for Checkerboards.

Makes about 5 dozen 3-inch cookies.

To Make Mosaics

1. Divide Light Dough in half. Transfer each half to a sheet of plastic wrap or waxed paper, and shape into a 2-inch-diameter log. Wrap each tightly and refrigerate until firm (at least 2 hours, or overnight; or place in freezer for 30 to 45 minutes).

2. Repeat procedure described in step 1 using Chocolate Dough.

3. Preheat oven to 350° F. Cut 1 roll each of Light Dough and Chocolate Dough into ¼-inch-thick slices. Use a small decorative cutter to remove center from each cookie slice. Place light centers in chocolate slices; place chocolate centers in light slices. Repeat with remaining rolls of dough. Bake as for Checkerboards.

Makes about 6 dozen 2½-inch cookies.

HONEY-ALMOND THINS

Any honey will flavor and gently sweeten these almond-studded cookies. But if you choose a distinctive floral honey, such as lavender or sage, the cookies will echo its aromatic overtones.

- 1½ *cups flour*
- 1 *teaspoon baking soda*
- ½ *cup butter or margarine, softened*
- ½ *cup vegetable shortening*
- ¾ *cup sugar*
- ½ *teaspoon vanilla extract*
- ¼ *teaspoon almond extract*
- 1 *teaspoon grated orange rind*
- ¼ *cup honey*
- 1 *cup slivered almonds*

1. In a bowl stir together flour and baking soda to combine thoroughly; set aside.

2. In mixer bowl beat butter, shortening, and sugar until well combined. Add vanilla, almond extract, and orange rind; beat until fluffy.

3. Add flour mixture alternately with honey, mixing to blend after each addition. Stir in almonds.

4. Transfer dough to a sheet of waxed paper or plastic wrap. Shape dough into two 2-inch-diameter logs. Enclose logs in waxed paper or plastic wrap and refrigerate until firm (at least 2 hours, or overnight; or place in freezer for 30 to 45 minutes).

5. Preheat oven to 350° F. Cut logs into ¼-inch-thick slices; arrange slices about 1½ inches apart on lightly greased baking sheets. Bake until cookies are golden brown (10 to 12 minutes). Let stand on baking sheets for about 2 minutes, then transfer to wire racks to cool.

Makes about 4 dozen 3-inch cookies.

CHOCOLATE TWEED COOKIES

Decorative sprinkles not only outline each of these cookies with chocolate, but are also dotted throughout the crisp fabric of the cookies.

- 1⅓ *cups flour*
- ½ *teaspoon baking powder*
- ¼ *teaspoon salt*
- ½ *cup butter or margarine, softened*
- ¼ *cup vegetable shortening*
- ½ *cup each granulated sugar and firmly packed brown sugar*
- ½ *teaspoon vanilla extract*
- 1 *egg yolk*
- ½ *cup finely chopped walnuts*
- ¾ *cup chocolate sprinkles*

1. In a bowl stir together flour, baking powder, and salt to combine thoroughly; set aside.

2. In mixer bowl combine butter and shortening; beat to blend well. Add sugars and beat until fluffy. Beat in vanilla, then egg yolk.

3. Gradually add flour mixture, beating until just blended. Stir in walnuts and ¼ cup of the chocolate sprinkles.

4. Spread ¼ cup of the remaining chocolate sprinkles on a piece of waxed paper or plastic wrap.

5. Divide dough in half. Transfer half to the chocolate-sprinkled paper; shape into a 1½-inch-diameter log evenly coated with sprinkles. Repeat with remaining chocolate sprinkles and cookie dough. Wrap each log tightly and refrigerate until firm (at least 2 hours, or overnight; or place in freezer for 30 to 45 minutes).

6. Preheat oven to 350° F. Remove one roll of cookie dough at a time from refrigerator and cut cookies into ¼-inch-thick slices. Arrange slices about 1 inch apart on ungreased baking sheets.

7. Bake until cookies are golden brown and feel firm when touched lightly (9 to 11 minutes). Let stand on baking sheets for about 2 minutes, then transfer to wire racks to cool.

Makes about fifty-four 2½-inch cookies.

CHERRY–CREAM-CHEESE SLICES

Chopped maraschino cherries lend a pastel pink tint and almond flavor to the tender-crisp cheese dough of these appealing refrigerator cookies.

- 1½ cups flour
- 1¼ teaspoon each *baking powder and baking soda*
- ⅛ teaspoon salt
- ½ cup *butter* or margarine, softened
- 1 small package (3 oz) cream cheese, softened
- ¾ cup sugar
- 1 teaspoon vanilla extract
- 1 egg yolk
- ½ cup chopped maraschino cherries

1. In a bowl stir together flour, baking powder, baking soda, and salt to combine thoroughly; set aside.

2. In mixer bowl combine butter and cream cheese; beat to blend well. Add sugar and beat until fluffy. Blend in vanilla, then egg yolk.

3. Gradually add flour mixture, beating until just blended. Stir in cherries.

4. Divide dough in half; transfer each half to a sheet of waxed paper or plastic wrap. Using a spatula and the paper, shape each half into a 2-inch-diameter log. Wrap each log tightly. Refrigerate until firm—at least 2 hours, or overnight (or place in freezer for 30 to 45 minutes).

5. Preheat oven to 350° F. Carefully slice logs into ¼-inch-thick slices; arrange slices, about 1 inch apart, on lightly greased baking sheets. Bake until cookies brown lightly (10 to 12 minutes). Transfer to wire racks to cool.

Makes about forty-two 2-inch cookies.

SOUR-CREAM–COCONUT WAFERS

Accompany these orange-accented, coconut-crisp cookies with a tart citrus sherbet for a refreshing dessert in warm weather. With rolls of dough waiting in the refrigerator, you can bake the cookies in the cool of the morning.

- 1½ cups flour
- ¼ teaspoon each *baking powder and baking soda*
- ⅛ teaspoon salt
- ½ cup *butter* or margarine, softened
- ½ cup each *granulated sugar and firmly packed brown sugar*
- 2 teaspoons grated orange rind
- 1 teaspoon vanilla extract
- 1 egg yolk
- ¼ cup sour cream
- 1½ cups flaked coconut

1. In a bowl stir together flour, baking powder, baking soda, and salt to combine thoroughly; set aside.

2. In mixer bowl beat butter and sugars until well combined; blend in orange rind and vanilla. Add egg yolk and sour cream; beat until fluffy.

3. Gradually add flour mixture, beating until just blended. Stir in coconut.

4. Divide dough in half; transfer each half to a sheet of waxed paper or plastic wrap. Using a spatula and the paper, shape each half into a 2-inch-diameter log. Wrap each log tightly. Refrigerate until firm—at least 2 hours, or overnight (or place in freezer for 30 to 45 minutes).

5. Preheat oven to 375° F. Cut logs into ¼-inch-thick slices; arrange slices, about 1 inch apart, on lightly greased baking sheets. Bake until cookies are golden (8 to 10 minutes). Transfer to wire racks to cool.

Makes about fifty-four 2½-inch cookies.

PINWHEELS

Pinwheel refrigerator cookies have filling spiraling through every slice. The cookie dough is chilled twice—once so it can be rolled out flat and again after filling is added and dough is rolled, jelly-roll style. The second chilling firms the dough and enables it to be sliced for baking.

The pattern of colors and flavors is so striking that it justifies the extra preparation time.

SWIRLED PEANUT BUTTER–FUDGE WAFERS

Peanut butter flavor fills both the rich chocolate cookie layer and the filling coiled inside it.

- 1 cup flour
- ¼ cup unsweetened cocoa
- ½ teaspoon baking soda
- ¼ teaspoon salt
- ½ cup *butter* or margarine, softened
- ½ cup peanut butter
- ½ cup each *granulated sugar and firmly packed brown sugar*
- 1 egg
- 1 package (6 oz) peanut butter chips

1. In a bowl stir together flour, cocoa, baking soda, and salt to combine thoroughly; set aside.

2. In mixer bowl combine butter and peanut butter; beat to blend well. Add sugars and beat until fluffy. Add egg and beat until well combined.

3. Gradually add flour mixture, beating until just blended. Enclose dough in plastic wrap and refrigerate until firm (1½ to 2 hours).

4. In a heavy pan over low heat, melt peanut butter chips; cool slightly.

5. Place dough between 2 sheets of plastic wrap, and roll into a 12- by 16-inch rectangle. Evenly spread melted peanut butter chips over dough to within ½ inch of edges. Starting with a 16-inch edge, use your fingers and the plastic wrap to roll dough, jelly-roll fashion. Roll tightly, removing plastic wrap as you roll. Cut roll in half to make two 8-inch-long rolls. Enclose each in plastic wrap and refrigerate for at least 3 hours, or overnight.

6. Preheat oven to 350° F. Remove one roll of cookie dough at a time from refrigerator; cut rolls into ¼-inch-thick slices. Arrange slices, about ½ inch apart, on ungreased baking sheets.

7. Bake until cookies feel firm when touched lightly (8 to 10 minutes). Let stand on baking sheets for about 2 minutes, then transfer to wire racks to cool completely.

Makes about fifty-four 2-inch cookies.

Swirled Peanut Butter–Fudge Wafers (at left) interface with Multicolored Refrigerator Cookies (see pages 84 and 85) in checkerboard, mosaic, and pinwheel patterns.

A crisp, brown-sugar cookie dough is wrapped around a ginger-spiced, dried-peach filling to make delicate Caramel-Peach Swirls.

CARAMEL-PEACH SWIRLS

Dried peaches spiced with ginger make a tart, moist filling for these buttery brown-sugar cookies.

- 1⅓ cups flour
- ½ teaspoon baking powder
- ¼ teaspoon salt
- ½ cup butter or margarine, softened
- ¼ cup vegetable shortening
- 1 cup firmly packed brown sugar
- ½ teaspoon vanilla extract
- 1 egg yolk

Ginger-Peach Filling

- 1 cup coarsely chopped dried peaches
- ½ cup water
- ⅓ cup sugar
- 1 tablespoon lemon juice
- ½ teaspoon ground ginger

1. In a bowl stir together flour, baking powder, and salt to combine thoroughly; set aside.

2. In mixer bowl combine butter and shortening; beat to blend well. Add brown sugar and beat until fluffy. Beat in vanilla, then egg yolk.

3. Gradually add flour mixture, beating until just blended. Enclose dough in plastic wrap and refrigerate until firm (about 2 hours).

4. Prepare Ginger-Peach Filling and let cool to room temperature.

5. Place dough between 2 sheets of plastic wrap, and roll into a 12- by 16-inch rectangle. Evenly spread filling over dough to within ½ inch of edges. Starting with a 16-inch edge, use your fingers and the plastic wrap to roll dough, jelly-roll fashion. Roll tightly, removing plastic wrap as you roll. Cut roll in half to make two 8-inch-long rolls. Enclose each in plastic wrap and refrigerate for at least 3 hours, or overnight.

6. Preheat oven to 350° F. Remove one roll of cookie dough at a time from refrigerator; cut rolls into ¼-inch-thick slices. Arrange slices about 1 inch apart on greased baking sheets.

7. Bake until cookies are golden brown and feel firm when touched lightly (8 to 10 minutes). Let stand on baking sheets for about 2 minutes, then transfer to wire racks to cool completely.

Makes about 5 dozen 2½-inch cookies.

Ginger-Peach Filling

1. In a small saucepan combine peaches, the water, sugar, lemon juice, and ginger. Place over medium heat and bring to a boil. Cover, reduce heat, and simmer until peaches are tender and most of liquid is absorbed (12 to 15 minutes). If necessary, uncover and cook for a few minutes longer to reduce liquid.

2. Transfer peach mixture to blender or food processor (or press through a food mill); whirl or process until coarsely puréed. Let stand at room temperature until cool.

CHOCOLATE-MINT PINWHEELS

Mint-flavored chocolate chips make a refreshing filling for these cookies.

- 1⅓ cups flour
- ½ teaspoon baking powder
- ¼ teaspoon salt
- ½ cup butter or margarine, softened
- ¼ cup vegetable shortening
- ½ cup each *granulated sugar and firmly packed brown sugar*
- 1 teaspoon vanilla extract
- 1 egg yolk
- 1 package (6 oz) mint-flavored chocolate chips

1. In a bowl stir together flour, baking powder, and salt to combine thoroughly; set aside.

2. In mixer bowl beat butter with shortening. Add sugars; beat until fluffy. Beat in vanilla, then egg yolk.

3. Gradually add flour mixture, beating until just blended. Enclose dough in plastic wrap and refrigerate until firm (1½ to 2 hours).

4. Place mint-flavored chocolate chips in a heavy pan over low heat until melted; cool slightly.

5. Place cookie dough between 2 sheets of plastic wrap and roll out to a 12- by 16-inch rectangle. Remove top sheet of plastic wrap. Spread melted chocolate evenly over dough to within ½ inch of edges. Starting with a 16-inch edge, roll dough tightly. Cut roll in half. Enclose each tightly in plastic wrap; refrigerate for at least 3 hours, or overnight.

6. Preheat oven to 350° F. Remove one roll of dough at a time from refrigerator; cut into ¼-inch-thick slices. Arrange slices about 1 inch apart on ungreased baking sheets.

7. Bake until cookies are golden brown and feel firm when touched lightly (8 to 10 minutes). Let stand on baking sheets for about 2 minutes, then transfer to wire racks to cool.

Makes about 5 dozen 2½-inch cookies.

Although the same cutter shapes them all, each Chocolate Malted Bear manages to take on a separate personality. The recipe for these cookies is on page 96.

Cutout Cookies

Rolling out and cutting a buttery dough into special shapes is a time-honored way of creating cookies. Tedious? Perhaps, yet such cookies have a way of evoking warm memories, and the process of making cutout cookies is a sweet way of enlisting willing helpers for the simpler tasks—even if it's only placing chocolate-chip smiles on the faces of rotund teddy-bear cookies.

ROLLED AND CUT COOKIES

Rolling out cookie dough and then cutting it into fanciful shapes brings out the artist in many bakers. Plan to make these cookies when interruptions are few. Prepare the rich, buttery dough, and wrap and refrigerate it on one day; then roll out, cut, and bake the cookies on the next.

TRADITIONAL SUGAR-COOKIE CUTOUTS

This classic cookie is rich, crisp, and faintly spiced—a perfect dough to cut into valentine hearts, George Washington hatchets, Easter chicks, Halloween pumpkins, or Christmas trees. To decorate them with colored icing, see page 99.

 1¾ cups flour
  2 teaspoons baking powder
  ¼ teaspoon ground mace
      or nutmeg
  ½ cup butter or margarine,
      softened
  1 cup sugar
  1 teaspoon vanilla extract
  1 egg
      Vanilla Granulated Sugar
      (see page 39), optional

1. In a bowl stir together flour, baking powder, and mace to combine thoroughly; set aside.

2. In mixer bowl combine butter and sugar; beat until light and fluffy. Blend in vanilla. Add egg and beat again until fluffy. Gradually add flour mixture, beating until just well combined.

3. Enclose dough in plastic wrap and refrigerate until firm (1 to 2 hours or overnight).

4. Preheat oven to 325° F. Work with about half of the dough at a time, keeping remainder in refrigerator. On a lightly floured board or pastry cloth, roll out dough to a thickness of about ⅛ inch. Cut with cookie cutters into rounds or other fancy shapes. Carefully transfer to lightly greased baking sheets. Sprinkle with Vanilla Granulated Sugar, if desired.

5. Bake until cookies are golden brown (10 to 12 minutes). Let stand for about 1 minute, then transfer to wire racks to cool.

Makes about 3 dozen cookies.

THIMBLE COOKIES

Use a thimble or other tiny cutter to create these brown-sugar cookies. Each makes a small mouthful, just right for a dolls' tea party or a teddy-bears' picnic. Cutting out the diminutive morsels will keep an aspiring young baker occupied for hours.

  ⅔ cup flour
  ¼ teaspoon baking powder
  ⅛ teaspoon ground cinnamon
  ¼ cup butter or margarine,
      softened
  ½ cup firmly packed brown
      sugar
  ¼ teaspoon vanilla extract
  1 egg yolk
  1 to 2 tablespoons dried
      currants

1. In a small bowl stir together flour, baking powder, and cinnamon to combine thoroughly; set aside.

2. In a medium bowl combine butter and brown sugar; beat with an electric mixer until well blended. Beat in vanilla and egg yolk. Gradually add flour mixture, beating until well combined.

3. Enclose dough in plastic wrap and refrigerate until firm (about 1 hour or overnight).

4. Preheat oven to 325° F. On a lightly floured board or pastry cloth, roll out dough to a thickness of about ⅛ inch. Cut with a thimble or other small, round cutter (¾ inch to 1 inch in diameter). Place cookies about ½ inch apart on ungreased baking sheets. Lightly press a currant into center of each.

5. Bake until cookies brown at edges (7 to 9 minutes). Transfer to wire racks to cool.

Makes about 10 dozen cookies.

JUMBLES

Fragrant rose water flavors these old-time favorite cookies, filling the room with its sweetness every time you open the oven. (You can find rose water at a pharmacy.) The cookies are cut into plump rings and decorated with chopped pecans.

 1¾ cups flour
  1 teaspoon baking powder
  ½ teaspoon ground nutmeg
  ¼ teaspoon salt
  ½ cup butter or margarine,
      softened
  ¾ cup granulated sugar
  1 egg
  1 tablespoon rose water
  ¼ cup (approximately)
      confectioners' sugar
  1 egg white, slightly beaten
      with 1 teaspoon each granu-
      lated sugar and water
  ¼ cup very finely chopped pecans

1. In a bowl stir together flour, baking powder, nutmeg, and salt to combine thoroughly; set aside.

2. In mixer bowl combine butter and granulated sugar; beat until light and fluffy. Add egg and beat again until fluffy; blend in rose water. Gradually add flour mixture, beating until just well combined.

3. Enclose dough in plastic wrap and refrigerate until firm (1 to 2 hours or overnight).

4. Preheat oven to 375° F. Work with about half of the dough at a time, keeping remainder in refrigerator. Lightly sprinkle a board or pastry cloth with confectioners' sugar; spread it to cover surface evenly. Roll out dough to a thickness of about ¼ inch, and cut with a 2¾-inch doughnut cutter. Carefully transfer rings to greased baking sheets.

5. Brush a little of the egg-white mixture over each cookie, then sprinkle with about ½ teaspoon pecans.

6. Bake until cookies are delicately browned (12 to 15 minutes). Cool on wire racks.

Makes about 2 dozen cookies.

Invite your best furry friends to a tea party with miniature Thimble Cookies and other teensy treats. Use a thimble to cut the petite rounds.

ENGLISH COUNTRY TEA

Caerphilly Biscuits

*Tiny Shrimp and
Chive Tarts*

*Watercress Finger
Sandwiches*

*Smoked Salmon Spread
on rye toast triangles*

Whole Strawberries

*Little Rascals
(see page 100)*

*Chocolate Butter-Cream
Sandwiches (see page 100)*

*Hot Tea, Lemon Slices,
Milk, Sugar*

Dry Sherry

---

*Finger foods are featured in
the array of temptations,
both savory and sweet, that
accompany a pot of hot tea
and a carafe of dry sherry.
Almost everything can be
made ahead; reheat the
cheese biscuits if you like.
Just before serving rinse the
berries, bake the shrimp
tarts, and make the fresh
toast to spread with the
smoked salmon butter.*

CAERPHILLY BISCUITS

1 cup flour
⅛ teaspoon each *paprika,
    dry mustard, and salt*
½ cup firm butter or margarine
1 cup (4 oz) shredded Caer-
    philly or white Cheddar cheese
1 egg yolk

1. In a bowl stir together flour, paprika, dry mustard, and salt to combine thoroughly.

2. Using a pastry blender or 2 knives, cut in butter and cheese until mixture resembles coarse crumbs. Add egg yolk; stir with a fork until dough clings together. Use your hands to press dough into a smooth ball. Enclose dough in plastic wrap and refrigerate until firm (at least 30 minutes).

3. Preheat oven to 400° F. On a lightly floured board or pastry cloth, roll out dough to a thickness of about ⅛ inch. Cut with a 1½- to 2-inch-diameter cutter. Place biscuits slightly apart on ungreased baking sheets. Pierce each in several places with a fork.

4. Bake until golden brown (10 to 12 minutes). Transfer to a wire rack to cool slightly, then serve warm or at room temperature.

Makes about 3 dozen 2-inch biscuits.

TINY SHRIMP AND CHIVE TARTS

1 sheet (half of a 17¼-oz
    package) frozen puff pastry
¼ pound tiny cooked shrimp
2 tablespoons mayonnaise
1 tablespoon chopped chives
1 teaspoon Dijon mustard
½ cup finely shredded Gruyère
    or Swiss cheese

1. Thaw puff pastry at room temperature for 30 minutes.

2. To prepare filling, combine shrimp, mayonnaise, chives, and mustard in a small bowl. Mix lightly to coat shrimp evenly.

3. On a lightly floured board or pastry cloth, unfold pastry and roll out to make an 11-inch square. Cut pastry with a 2-inch-diameter cutter. Lightly press each pastry round over bottom and partway up sides of an ungreased cup of a 1¾-inch muffin pan. (Press pastry trimmings together lightly, roll out, and cut until most of pastry is used.)

4. Fill each pastry shell with 2 or 3 shrimp. Sprinkle with a rounded ½ teaspoon of cheese. Refrigerate for at least 30 minutes or up to 2 hours.

5. Preheat oven to 450° F. Bake tarts until pastry is golden brown (12 to 14 minutes). Remove at once from pans and serve hot.

Makes 3 dozen tarts.

WATERCRESS FINGER SANDWICHES

¼ cup butter or margarine,
    softened
2 tablespoons cream cheese,
    softened
1 teaspoon Dijon mustard
1 cup lightly packed watercress
    leaves
6 thin slices firm-textured
    white bread

1. In a food-processor work bowl, combine butter, cream cheese, mustard, and watercress. Process until well combined.

2. Trim and discard crusts from bread. Spread half of the slices evenly with watercress mixture; cover with remaining slices. Cut each sandwich into 3 equal strips.

3. If sandwiches are made ahead, enclose in plastic wrap and refrigerate until ready to serve (up to 8 hours).

Makes 18 sandwiches.

SMOKED SALMON SPREAD

3 ounces smoked salmon or
  lox, coarsely chopped

1 egg yolk

1 tablespoon lemon juice

1 teaspoon chopped fresh
  dill or ¼ teaspoon dried
  dill weed

⅛ teaspoon white pepper

¼ cup butter or margarine
  (preferably unsalted), melted
  and cooled

Rye or pumpernickel toast

1. In a food processor or blender, combine smoked salmon, egg yolk, lemon juice, dill, and white pepper; process or whirl until smooth.

2. With motor running, add melted butter in a steady stream, blending until thickened and smooth. Transfer mixture to a crock or bowl, cover, and refrigerate to blend flavors for at least 1 hour or up to a day.

3. To serve, spread over warm triangles of toast.

Makes about ⅔ cup.

Small, savory tidbits and delicate sandwich cookies complement hot tea or dry sherry at teatime. Recipes for Little Rascals and Chocolate Butter-Cream Sandwiches are on page 100.

95

CHOCOLATE MALTED BEARS

Fancifully decorated with miniature chocolate chips, these thin, crisp cookies will be a hit with teddy-bear fanciers of all ages. If you do not already have a bear-shaped cutter, it is worth acquiring one in order to make these charmers.

    1½ cups flour
    ¼ cup chocolate malted-milk powder
    1 teaspoon baking powder
    ½ cup butter or margarine, softened
    ½ cup each granulated sugar and firmly packed brown sugar
    1 teaspoon vanilla extract
    1 egg
    2 tablespoons (approximately) miniature semisweet chocolate chips

1. In a bowl stir together flour, malted milk powder, and baking powder to combine well; set aside.

2. In mixer bowl combine butter and sugars; beat until light and fluffy. Blend in vanilla. Add egg and beat again until fluffy. Gradually add flour mixture, beating until just well combined.

3. Enclose dough in plastic wrap and refrigerate until firm (1 to 2 hours or overnight).

4. Preheat oven to 325° F. Work with about half of the dough at a time, keeping remainder in refrigerator. On a lightly floured board or pastry cloth, roll out dough to a thickness of about ⅛ inch. Cut with a 3½-inch-tall bear-shaped cookie cutter. Transfer cookies to ungreased baking sheets. Decorate bears with miniature chocolate chips as desired.

5. Bake until cookies begin to brown and feel firm when touched lightly (10 to 12 minutes). Let stand for about 1 minute, then transfer to wire racks to cool.

Makes about 4 dozen cookies.

SPICY APPLES

Apple-pie spice flavors these crisp, apple-shaped cookies. Serve them with warm, homemade applesauce for a double-apple dessert.

    2 cups flour
    1 tablespoon apple-pie spice
    ½ teaspoon baking powder
    ⅛ teaspoon salt
    ¼ cup ground unblanched almonds
    ¾ cup butter or margarine, softened
    1 cup firmly packed brown sugar
    1 to 2 tablespoons apple juice or cider

1. In a bowl stir together flour, apple-pie spice, baking powder, salt, and almonds; set aside.

2. In mixer bowl combine butter and brown sugar; beat until light and fluffy. Blend in 1 tablespoon of the apple juice. Gradually add flour mixture, beating until just well combined. (If dough is too crumbly to cling together, blend in up to 1 tablespoon more apple juice.)

3. Enclose dough in plastic wrap and refrigerate until firm (1 to 2 hours or overnight).

4. Preheat oven to 350° F. Work with about half of the dough at a time, keeping remainder in refrigerator. On a lightly floured board or pastry cloth, roll out dough to a thickness of about ⅛ inch. Cut with an apple-shaped cutter about 2¾ inches in diameter. Place cookies about 1 inch apart on ungreased baking sheets.

5. Bake until cookies feel firm when touched lightly and edges are brown (10 to 12 minutes). Transfer to wire racks to cool.

Makes about 3 dozen cookies.

FILLED COOKIES

Adding a filling to cutout cookies makes them all the more tempting. There's more than one way to go about it—as shown in the following recipes.

The fillings, as well as the doughs, for both the turnovers (page 98) and the ravioli (page 99) can be made ahead, but wait to whip up the meringue centers for the pastry cookies (recipe below) until shortly before you bake them.

MERINGUE-FILLED COOKIE PASTRIES

Cookies for breakfast? These crisp and flaky little pastries of Eastern European origin may remind you of Danish pastry, although the tangy, sour cream–enriched yeast dough is much easier to make. If cookies in the morning sound too rich to you, they're also good with a steaming cup of coffee at any time of the day or evening.

    1 package active dry yeast
    ¼ cup warm (105° to 115°F) water
    3 cups flour
    ½ teaspoon salt
    2 egg yolks
    ⅔ cup sour cream
    1 teaspoon vanilla extract
    ¾ cup firm butter or margarine
    ½ cup (approximately) confectioners' sugar

Meringue Filling

    2 egg whites
    ½ cup granulated sugar
    1 teaspoon vanilla extract
    ¼ cup each fine, dry bread crumbs and very finely chopped walnuts

1. In a medium bowl sprinkle yeast over the water. Let stand until yeast is soft (about 5 minutes).

2. In a large bowl stir together flour and salt to combine well; set aside.

3. To yeast mixture add egg yolks, sour cream, and vanilla. Beat with a whisk until well blended; set aside.

4. Using a pastry blender or 2 knives, cut butter into flour mixture until coarse crumbs form. Add yeast mixture to flour mixture, stirring until flour is evenly moistened.

5. Enclose dough in plastic wrap and refrigerate until firm (at least 2 hours, or overnight).

6. Preheat oven to 350° F. Work with a third of the dough at a time, keeping remainder in refrigerator. Sprinkle a board or pastry cloth with some of the confectioners' sugar, rubbing it in evenly. Roll out dough to a 10-inch square.

7. Using a pastry wheel or knife, cut dough into 2½-inch squares. Spoon about 1 teaspoon of Meringue Filling into center of each square. Bring up 2 opposite corners to overlap slightly in center, firmly pinching them together to seal. Place pastries about 2 inches apart on lightly greased baking sheets. Repeat with remaining dough.

8. Bake until golden brown (18 to 20 minutes). Transfer to wire racks to cool. Sift a little more confectioners' sugar over cooled cookies, if desired.

Makes 4 dozen cookies.

Meringue Filling Beat egg whites at high speed until stiff peaks form. Gradually add sugar, beating until meringue is stiff and glossy. Blend in vanilla. Combine bread crumbs and walnuts; fold into meringue.

Unusual because they're made from a yeast dough, Meringue-Filled Cookie Pastries are delicious for breakfast with freshly squeezed blood-orange juice, plump strawberries, and coffee or tea.

Fresh, tropical fruits and sugar-sprinkled Lime-Coconut Turnovers are an ideal conclusion to a Mexican- or Caribbean-style dinner.

LIME-COCONUT TURNOVERS

With a tart, fresh-lime filling, these empanada-style cookies have a Mexican spirit. They're a good dessert to serve with fresh fruit as the conclusion to a south-of-the-border dinner.

  1½ cups flour
  1½ teaspoons baking powder
  2 tablespoons sugar
  ¼ teaspoon each *salt* and *ground cinnamon*
  ¼ cup firm butter or margarine
  2 tablespoons lard or vegetable shortening
  2½ to 3 tablespoons cold water
  2 teaspoons (approximately) milk
  2 tablespoons (approximately) Vanilla Granulated Sugar (see page 39)

Lime-Coconut Filling

  1 egg
  ⅓ cup sugar
  ½ teaspoon grated lime rind
  2 tablespoons lime juice
  1 tablespoon butter or margarine
  2 tablespoons flaked coconut

1. In a bowl stir together flour, baking powder, sugar, salt, and cinnamon to combine thoroughly. Using a pastry blender or 2 knives, cut in butter and lard until mixture resembles coarse crumbs.

2. Add the cold water, 1 tablespoon at a time, mixing lightly with a fork until dough clings together. Use your hands to press dough into a smooth ball. Enclose dough in plastic wrap and refrigerate until firm (about 1 hour or overnight).

3. On a lightly floured board or pastry cloth, roll out dough to a thickness of a scant ⅛ inch. Using a 3¼- to 3½-inch-diameter cutter, cut dough into circles.

4. Preheat oven to 375° F. Place about 2 teaspoons of Lime-Coconut Filling on half of each circle, leaving about ½ inch at edge uncovered. Moisten edge of each circle with tap water. Fold over unfilled half, and press edges together with tines of a fork to seal.

5. Place turnovers about 2 inches apart on greased baking sheets. Brush top of each with milk, then sprinkle with Vanilla Granulated Sugar.

6. Bake until lightly browned (15 to 18 minutes). Transfer to wire racks to cool.

Makes 14 to 16 cookies.

Lime-Coconut Filling Beat egg in a small, heavy saucepan. Stir in sugar, lime rind, and lime juice. Add butter and place over low heat. Cook, stirring often, until mixture thickens (6 to 8 minutes). Remove from heat and stir in coconut. Let stand at room temperature for 15 to 20 minutes to cool.

APRICOT-FILLED COOKIE RAVIOLI

Including cornstarch in the dough of these sugar-dusted cookies makes the pastry both crisp and tender. Use a pastry wheel to cut the filled cookie squares, cutting between the mounds of filling just as if making ravioli.

  1¾ *cups flour*
  ½ *cup cornstarch*
  ¼ *teaspoon ground nutmeg*
  ½ *cup butter or margarine, softened*
  ½ *cup sugar*
  1 *teaspoon each vanilla extract and grated lemon rind*
  1 *tablespoon grappa, brandy, or lemon juice*
  1 *egg*
    Vanilla Confectioners' Sugar (see page 39)

Apricot Filling

  ⅔ *cup coarsely chopped dried apricots*
  ¼ *cup water*
  ⅓ *cup sugar*
  1 *tablespoon grappa, brandy, or Marsala wine*

1. In a bowl stir together flour, cornstarch, and nutmeg to combine thoroughly; set aside.

2. In mixer bowl combine butter and sugar; beat until light and fluffy. Beat in vanilla, lemon rind, and grappa. Add egg and beat again until fluffy. Gradually add flour mixture, beating until just well combined. Enclose dough in plastic wrap and refrigerate until firm (about 2 hours or overnight).

3. Preheat oven to 350° F. Divide dough into 4 equal parts; return 3 parts to refrigerator. On a well-floured board or pastry cloth, roll out dough to a 6- by 12-inch strip. Spoon about ½-teaspoon portions of Apricot Filling in rows across dough at 2-inch intervals.

4. Roll out another fourth of the dough to a 6- by 12-inch strip. Place over filled strip. With your floured finger, press down between mounds of filling to seal dough; press outer edges to seal. Using a pastry wheel or knife, cut between mounds of filling to make 2-inch squares. Place filled squares slightly apart on greased baking sheets. Repeat with remaining dough.

5. Bake until cookies feel firm when touched lightly and edges are brown (12 to 15 minutes).

6. Transfer to wire racks. While cookies are still warm, sprinkle with Vanilla Confectioners' Sugar.

Makes 3 dozen 2-inch-square cookies.

Apricot Filling

1. In a small saucepan combine apricots, water, and sugar. Place over high heat and bring to a boil, stirring until sugar dissolves. Cover, reduce heat, and simmer until apricots are tender and most of the liquid is absorbed (8 to 10 minutes). If necessary, uncover and cook for a few minutes longer to reduce liquid. Mix in grappa.

2. Transfer apricot mixture to a blender or food processor (or press through a food mill); whirl or process until coarsely puréed. Let stand at room temperature until cool.

Step·by·Step

FROSTING CUTOUT COOKIES

1. *Attach decorating tip of your choice to pastry bag. Twist bag just above tip and push twisted portion into tip (this prevents icing from running out while you are filling bag). Fold down top of bag to form cuff. Fill bag no more than half full with frosting of your choice.*

2. *To decorate with frosting, unfold cuff and press sides of bag together at top, running your fingers down the outside of bag to force frosting into lower half. Untwist small end of bag. Gently squeeze frosting from top, using your other hand to guide bag. Periodically twist bag to increase pressure on frosting and keep it moving evenly through tip.*

Step-by-Step

SANDWICH COOKIES

1. *With a small spatula spread Butter-Cream Filling on half of chocolate cookies. Top each with plain cookie.*

2. *Fit pastry bag with plain, round tip. For Little Rascals fill bag with apricot jam; pipe jam onto half of cookies. Top each with plain cookie.*

3. *Place frozen disks of mint ice cream between plain and chocolate-drizzled cookies to make Grasshopper Ice Cream Sandwiches. Freeze; wrap individually in foil to store.*

SANDWICH COOKIES

Rolled and cutout cookies are perfect for making tempting sandwich cookies, because you can design their size, shape, and thickness with your choice of a cutter and a twirl of the rolling pin. Filled with jam or jelly, a creamy icing, or even ice cream, these sweet treats can be as varied as your imagination.

LITTLE RASCALS

Nutmeg flecked and bite-sized, these buttery, apricot-filled morsels are of Dutch origin. It is best to assemble the sandwiches no more than two hours before serving, because the cookies may absorb moisture from the filling and soften after standing for several hours. The baked cookies can be kept on hand in the freezer; making them into sandwiches is quick when you use a pastry bag to apply the apricot-jam centers.

> 1¼ cups flour
> ⅓ cup sugar
> ⅛ teaspoon ground nutmeg
> ½ cup firm butter or magarine
> 1 egg yolk
> ½ teaspoon vanilla extract
> ⅓ to ½ cup apricot jam or preserves
> Vanilla Confectioners' Sugar (see page 39)

1. In a medium bowl combine flour, sugar, and nutmeg; stir to blend thoroughly. Using a pastry blender or 2 knives, cut in butter until mixture forms coarse crumbs.

2. In a small bowl beat egg yolk with vanilla. Stir egg mixture into flour mixture until all particles are moistened. Work with your hands to form dough into a smooth ball. Enclose in plastic wrap and refrigerate until firm (about 1 hour).

3. Preheat oven to 400° F. On a lightly floured board or pastry cloth, roll out dough to a thickness of about ⅛ inch. Cut out cookies with a 1¼- to 1½-inch-diameter cutter. Transfer to ungreased baking sheets.

4. Bake until cookies are golden (6 to 8 minutes). Transfer to wire racks to cool.

5. Fill a pastry bag, fitted with a plain round tip, with jam. Apply about ¾ teaspoon jam to half of the cookies. Cover each with a plain cookie. Just before serving, sift lightly with Vanilla Confectioners' Sugar.

Makes about 40 cookies.

CHOCOLATE BUTTER-CREAM SANDWICHES

A flaky, tender chocolate pastry makes these delicate cookies irresistible. The fluffy cream filling tastes as though its preparation is more complex than it actually is.

> 1 cup flour
> 2 tablespoons unsweetened cocoa
> ½ cup firm butter or margarine
> 2 tablespoons whipping cream
> 2 tablespoons (approximately) confectioners' sugar

Butter-Cream Filling

> 3 tablespoons butter or margarine, softened
> ¾ cup confectioners' sugar
> 2 to 3 teaspoons whipping cream
> ½ teaspoon vanilla extract

1. In a medium bowl combine flour and cocoa; stir to combine thoroughly. Using a pastry blender or 2 knives, cut in butter until mixture forms coarse crumbs.

2. Stir in cream, 1 tablespoon at a time, until all particles are moistened. Work with your hands to form mixture into a smooth ball. Enclose in plastic wrap and refrigerate until firm (about 1 hour).

3. Preheat oven to 375° F. Sprinkle a board with confectioners' sugar, rubbing it in evenly. Roll out dough to a thickness of about ⅛ inch. Cut out cookies with a 1¼- to 1½-inch-diameter cutter. Transfer to lightly greased baking sheets. Use a fork to pierce each cookie in 2 or 3 places.

4. Bake until cookies feel firm when touched lightly (8 to 10 minutes). Let cool on baking sheets for about 2 minutes, then carefully transfer to wire racks to cool.

5. Using a small spatula, spread half of the cookies with Butter-Cream Filling, using about 1 teaspoon for each. Cover with plain cookies.

Makes about 3 dozen cookies.

Butter-Cream Filling In a small bowl combine butter and sugar; beat until well blended. Gradually beat in cream, then vanilla, until filling is smooth and of a good spreading consistency.

GRASSHOPPER ICE CREAM SANDWICHES

The popular combination of chocolate and mint flavors is hard to beat.

- ⅔ cup flour
- 3 tablespoons unsweetened cocoa
- ¼ teaspoon each *baking soda and salt*
- ½ cup butter or margarine, softened
- ¾ cup sugar
- 1 egg yolk
- ½ teaspoon vanilla extract
- 2 tablespoons water
- 1½ cups quick-cooking rolled oats
- 1 square (1 oz) semisweet baking chocolate
- ½ teaspoon salad oil
- 1 quart (approximately) mint chocolate-chip or mint chocolate-ripple ice cream

1. In a bowl stir together flour, cocoa, baking soda, and salt to combine thoroughly; set aside.

2. In mixer bowl combine butter and sugar; beat until fluffy. Beat in egg yolk. Add vanilla and mix to blend.

3. Add flour mixture alternately with the water, blending until smooth after each addition. Stir in rolled oats. Enclose dough in plastic wrap and refrigerate until firm (about 1 hour).

4. Preheat oven to 350° F. On a lightly floured board or pastry cloth, roll out dough to a thickness of about ⅛ inch. Cut out cookies with a 2½-inch-diameter cutter. Transfer to ungreased baking sheets.

5. Bake until cookies are barely firm when touched lightly (8 to 10 minutes). Let stand on baking sheets for 1 to 2 minutes, then remove to wire racks to cool.

6. While cookies are cooling, melt semisweet chocolate with oil in a small, heavy pan over low heat. Over half the cookies drizzle melted chocolate from a paper cone (see page 109) or the tip of a teaspoon; set aside until chocolate is firm.

7. With an ice cream scoop, place 15 mounds of ice cream on a shallow-rimmed baking sheet. Use a spatula to flatten each scoop to about a 3-inch-diameter disk. Return ice cream to freezer until solidly frozen (1 to 2 hours).

8. To assemble sandwiches place plain cookies, smooth sides up, in rows on a shallow-rimmed baking sheet. Place a disk of the ice cream atop each. Cover each with a chocolate-drizzled cookie, chocolate side up. Return to freezer until ice cream sandwiches are solidly frozen (1 to 2 hours). To store, individually wrap sandwiches in foil. Cookies can be kept in freezer for up to 2 months.

Makes 15 ice cream sandwiches.

Mint-flecked ice cream is sandwiched between chocolate-oatmeal cookies drizzled with chocolate to make Grasshopper Ice Cream Sandwiches. They are a wonderful treat— and one that can be accomplished well in advance—for a birthday celebration.

It wouldn't be Christmas without cookies, and one of the most classic is Spritz—chocolate or vanilla (see page 115).

Holiday Cookies

You don't have to wait for a holiday to make these splendid cookies, but some holidays clearly wouldn't be the same without them. Spritz (see page 115) means Christmas in almost all of northern Europe, and what American Christmas would be complete without gingerbread? All over the world, the aroma of spices and toasted nuts marks the holiday kitchen, signaling the presence of good food in the making. The world's best-known holiday cookies range from the Rugelach (see page 119) of Hanukkah to the German Pfeffernüsse (see page 104) of Christmas. Recipes for these and other favorites are in the chapter that follows.

CHRISTMAS COOKIES FROM AROUND THE WORLD

Wherever Christmas is celebrated, cooks have created a repertoire of special sweets to honor the season.

In some countries, cookie baking starts weeks before Christmas. Dried and candied fruits, nuts, spices, and pounds of butter fill the larder, to be turned into wreaths, rings, bars, stars and—of course—gingerbread.

The following pages offer an international array of Christmas cookies.

GINGERBREAD PEOPLE

It wouldn't be Christmas without these little cookie people, thickly cut from a spicy molasses dough. Make a batch for a children's party and encourage children to decorate their own. School-age children can maneuver an icing-filled paper cone (see page 109). For younger children, provide a confectioners' sugar glaze (see page 118), decorating sugar, and sugar sprinkles.

- ½ cup unsalted butter, softened
- ½ cup firmly packed brown sugar
- ½ cup molasses
- 1 egg
- 2½ cups flour
- 1 teaspoon baking soda
- ½ teaspoon salt
- 2 teaspoons ground ginger
- 1 teaspoon ground cinnamon
- ½ teaspoon ground nutmeg
- ½ teaspoon ground cloves
  Dried currants, for decorating

Royal Icing I

- 1¼ cups sifted confectioners' sugar
- 1 egg white
- 1 teaspoon strained lemon juice
  Food coloring (optional)

1. In large mixer bowl cream butter; gradually add sugar and beat until light. Add molasses and egg and beat to blend well; set aside.

2. In a bowl stir together flour, baking soda, salt, ginger, cinnamon, nutmeg, and cloves. Gradually add flour mixture to butter mixture, beating until just blended. Gather dough into a ball and enclose in plastic wrap; refrigerate at least 1 hour.

3. Preheat oven to 325° F. On a lightly floured board, roll out gingerbread to a thickness of ¼ inch. Cut out cookies with a floured, 4½-inch-long cutter and transfer to greased baking sheets. Bake until cookies are lightly browned around edges and feel barely firm when touched gently (about 10 minutes). Transfer to wire racks. While each cookie is hot, press in currants to create eyes, mouth, and buttons. When cool, decorate with Royal Icing I piped from a paper cone (see page 109).

Makes about 1 dozen 4-inch-long cookies.

Royal Icing I In a small bowl combine ¾ cup of the sugar with egg white and lemon juice. Beat until thick and white (about 10 minutes). Add remaining sugar and beat until stiff. Tint icing with food coloring, if desired.

Makes ¾ cup.

SCOTTISH YULE BANNOCK

To distinguish their Christmas shortbread from the kind they make all year, some Scottish bakers add minced almonds and candied citron to the dough. This Yule bannock (bread) is cut into bite-sized cubes after baking. The butter-rich cookies literally melt in your mouth.

- 1½ cups flour
- ¼ teaspoon salt
- ⅜ cup confectioners' sugar
- ⅓ cup finely minced, candied citron or mixed candied fruit
- ¼ cup finely minced, toasted almonds (see page 29)
- ¾ cup unsalted butter, cut into pieces and slightly softened
- 1½ tablespoons granulated sugar

1. Preheat oven to 325° F. *To prepare in a food processor:* In work bowl of food processor, combine flour, salt, and confectioners' sugar.

Pulse briefly until just blended. Add citron, almonds, and butter. Pulse several times until mixture resembles fine crumbs. *To prepare by hand:* On a cool work surface, combine flour, salt, and sugar; stir to blend. Add citron and almonds; toss to coat citron with flour mixture. Cut in butter with pastry blender or 2 knives until mixture resembles fine crumbs.

2. Lightly press dough into an 8-inch-square baking pan, then sprinkle with granulated sugar. Bake until lightly browned (about 30 minutes). Immediately cut into 64 squares. Let cool in pan 10 minutes, then transfer to a wire rack to finish cooling.

Makes 64 cookies.

PFEFFERNÜSSE

The traditional *Pfeffernüsse* is dotted with brandy just before baking to cause it to puff and form a topknot. Make these cookies several weeks before Christmas. They have a rock-hard texture at first; allow the cookies to mellow for three weeks in a tightly covered container. Add a slice of apple to the container to soften the cookies a day before serving them.

- 2 eggs
- ½ cup granulated sugar
- ½ cup firmly packed brown sugar
  Grated rind of 1 lemon
- ¼ cup finely ground almonds
- 2 tablespoons minced candied fruit
- 2 cups sifted flour
- ½ teaspoon baking powder
- ½ teaspoon ground cinnamon
- ¼ teaspoon freshly ground pepper
- ¼ teaspoon each ground cloves, ginger, and cardamom
- ⅛ to ¼ cup (approximately) brandy
  Sifted confectioners' sugar, for coating

1. In large mixer bowl beat eggs with whisk attachment until light. Gradually add sugars; whisk at high speed for 10 minutes.

2. Replace whisk attachment with a paddle. Beat in lemon rind, almonds, and candied fruit; set aside.

3. In a bowl sift together flour, baking powder, cinnamon, pepper, cloves, ginger, and cardamom. On lowest speed gradually add flour mixture to egg mixture, beating until just blended.

4. Turn dough onto a lightly floured board. With your floured hands, pat dough to a thickness of ¼ inch. Cut with a lightly floured, 1-inch-round cutter. Place cookies 1 inch apart on greased and floured baking sheets. Let cookies stand uncovered in a cool place several hours or overnight.

5. Preheat oven to 300° F. Turn over cookies. Use your finger to sprinkle a drop of brandy onto center of each. Bake until cookies puff and are no longer sticky inside (about 20 minutes). Break one open to make sure it is done in center. Transfer to wire racks and let cool slightly. When cookies are barely warm, shake them in a bag with sifted confectioners' sugar. Store in an airtight container for at least 3 weeks before eating.

Makes about 5 dozen cookies.

A paper cone filled with white icing transforms faceless Gingerbread People into your own Christmas creations. They're as much fun to bake and decorate as they are to eat.

105

*Crisp, meringue-topped
Cinnamon Stars, made from a
flourless almond dough,
are a holiday classic in their
native Germany.*

CINNAMON STARS

Crunchy German *Zimtsterne* (cinnamon stars) contain no flour or fat. They are a meringue-based cookie, the meringue made stiff with ground almonds. The sticky dough is easier to pat out than to roll and can be cut into other shapes as well.

      3 egg whites, at room
         temperature
         Pinch salt
   1¼ cups superfine sugar
      1 tablespoon ground cinnamon
      5 to 5½ cups (approximately)
         finely ground unblanched
         almonds

1. In mixer bowl beat egg whites with salt to soft peaks. Gradually add sugar; beat at high speed 10 minutes. With a spoon remove ¾ cup of the meringue and set aside. Using lowest speed, add cinnamon to remaining meringue and beat thoroughly.

2. Add 4½ cups of the ground almonds to meringue, folding them in gently but thoroughly.

3. Pat out dough to a thickness of about ¼ inch. On a work surface sprinkled with the remaining ½ to 1 cup ground almonds (use as needed to keep dough from sticking), cut dough with a star-shaped cutter. Transfer cookies to greased and floured baking sheets.

4. Using a pastry brush or table knife, paint top of each cookie with an even layer of reserved meringue. Let cookies stand in a cool place for 2 hours.

5. When cookies are almost cool, preheat oven to 300° F. Bake until cookies are very lightly colored and tops feel firm when touched gently (about 20 minutes). Cool 5 minutes on baking sheets, then transfer to wire racks to cool completely. Store in an airtight container.

Makes about 2 dozen 3-inch cookies.

TOFFEE DIAMONDS

Few cookies are easier to make than these crunchy Toffee Diamonds. The toffee base can be assembled in minutes, and the chocolate chips for the glaze are melted directly on the hot cookies. Watch the dough carefully as it bakes. It must cook until well browned to bring out the crisp toffee character, but it quickly goes from browned to burned.

      1 cup unsalted butter, softened
      1 cup firmly packed
         brown sugar
   ¼ teaspoon salt
   ½ teaspoon vanilla extract
      1 egg yolk
      1 cup flour
      1 package (8 oz) semisweet
         chocolate chips
   ¼ cup minced, toasted walnuts
         (see page 29)

1. Preheat oven to 350° F. In large bowl of electric mixer, cream butter, sugar, salt, vanilla, and egg yolk until smooth. Gradually add flour, beating until just blended.

2. Spread mixture evenly in a greased, shallow 10¼- by 15¼-inch baking pan. Bake until well browned (about 15 to 20 minutes); watch carefully to prevent burning.

3. Remove from oven and sprinkle chocolate chips evenly over surface. Let pan cool on wire rack 10 minutes while chocolate chips melt, then spread them evenly over surface with a spatula. Garnish with walnuts. Let cool completely before slicing into diamonds.

Makes about forty-five 1½-inch cookies.

THUMBPRINTS

Despite their name, these butter-rich cookies are best shaped with a thimble. Fill the hollows with your favorite jam or a colorful assortment of jams.

   ¼ cup toasted pecans
         (see page 29)
   ½ cup unsalted butter, softened
   ¼ cup firmly packed
         brown sugar
      1 egg yolk
   ½ teaspoon vanilla extract
   ½ teaspoon salt
      1 cup sifted flour
      4 tablespoons (approximately)
         apricot and/or raspberry jam

1. Grind toasted pecans in blender until fine but not powdery; set aside.

2. In large mixer bowl cream butter; add brown sugar and beat until light and fluffy. Add egg yolk and blend well. Beat in vanilla and salt. Add flour by hand, stirring until just blended. Gather dough into a ball and enclose in waxed paper; refrigerate several hours or overnight.

3. Preheat oven to 350° F. Work with one half of dough at a time, keeping remainder in refrigerator. Divide unrefrigerated dough into 12 equal pieces. With your lightly floured hands, roll each piece into a ball. Place balls on an ungreased baking sheet. Repeat with other half of dough. Using a lightly floured thimble, make a small, deep indentation in the center of each cookie.

4. Bake 10 minutes, then remove cookies from oven and press indentations down again. Fill each with about ½ teaspoon jam. Return to oven and bake until cookies are lightly browned around edges (3 to 4 minutes). Cool on wire racks.

Makes 2 dozen 1¼-inch cookies.

FRUITCAKE DROPS

These are a fruitcake lover's dream: plenty of rum-soaked fruits and nuts with just enough batter to hold them together.

   ¾ cup dark raisins
   ¾ cup golden raisins
   1 cup chopped pitted dates
   1 cup chopped, mixed candied
      fruit
   ½ cup dark rum
   2 cups flour
   ½ teaspoon baking soda
   ½ teaspoon ground cinnamon
   ¼ teaspoon salt
   ½ cup unsalted butter, softened
   ½ cup firmly packed brown
      sugar
   2 eggs
   2 cups toasted pecan
      halves, coarsely chopped
      (see page 29)
   1 cup toasted, slivered
      almonds (see page 29)
      Confectioners' sugar,
      for dusting (optional)

1. In a large bowl combine raisins, dates, candied fruit, and rum. Stir to blend. Transfer to a lidded jar; macerate at room temperature for 24 hours, shaking jar occasionally.

2. Preheat oven to 300° F. In a medium bowl stir together flour, baking soda, cinnamon, and salt. Set aside.

3. In large bowl of electric mixer, cream butter; gradually add brown sugar and beat until light. Add eggs, one at a time, blending well after each addition. Add macerated fruit and beat to blend. On lowest speed add flour mixture, beating until just blended. Stir in nuts by hand.

4. Drop dough by generous tablespoons, placed about 1½ inches apart, onto greased baking sheets. Bake until lightly browned on bottom (about 15 to 18 minutes). Transfer to wire racks. When cool, sift confectioners' sugar over cookies, if desired.

Makes about fifty 2-inch cookies.

ARISTOCRATS

Danish Christmas baking includes a variety of butter cookies, but few are as tempting as these. They are a two-in-one treat: nut or chocolate dough, formed into a log, is encased in vanilla dough and rolled in sugar. The sliced cookies reveal their pattern, which always charms guests.

   14 tablespoons unsalted butter,
       softened
   ⅔ cup granulated sugar
   2 eggs
   1 teaspoon vanilla extract
   2½ cups flour
   ⅓ cup finely minced almonds
      or pecans
   1½ ounces bittersweet chocolate,
       finely minced
       Coarse sugar (pearl or
       decorating sugar, or crushed
       sugar cubes), for coating

1. In a large mixing bowl cream butter; gradually add granulated sugar and beat until light. Add one of the eggs and vanilla; beat well. Gradually add flour, beating until just blended.

2. Divide dough in half; enclose one half in waxed paper or plastic wrap and refrigerate. Divide other half in half again. Add almonds to one part, kneading to blend well; add chocolate to other part and knead to blend well. With your lightly floured hands, roll each part into a 10-inch-long log.

3. On a lightly floured board, roll refrigerated dough into a 9-inch by 11-inch rectangle. Beat remaining egg and lightly brush on dough. Cut dough in half to make 2 rectangles, each 4½ inches by 11 inches. Position nut log in center of 1 rectangle and chocolate log in center of other. Wrap logs securely with plain dough, pressing seams together and sealing ends. Lightly brush each log all over with beaten egg; roll in coarse sugar. Wrap each log in aluminum foil; refrigerate several hours.

4. Preheat oven to 400° F. Cut each log into 36 slices. Place, about 1 inch apart, on ungreased baking sheets. Bake until bottoms are lightly browned (about 10 minutes). Transfer to wire racks to cool. Store in airtight containers.

Makes 6 dozen 1¾-inch cookies.

PECAN PRALINE ROUNDS

Pecans, cream, and sugar combine to make a praline topping for these irresistible buttery rounds.

   ½ cup unsalted butter, softened
   1 cup plus 1 tablespoon sugar
   1 egg
   1½ teaspoons vanilla extract
   1¾ cups flour
   2 teaspoons baking powder
   ¼ teaspoon salt
   ⅔ cup whipping cream
   1 cup finely chopped toasted
      pecans (see page 29)
      Sugar, for flattening cookies

1. In mixer bowl cream butter; gradually add 1 cup of the sugar and beat until light. Add egg and vanilla and beat thoroughly; set aside.

2. In a bowl stir together flour, baking powder, and salt. Gradually add to butter mixture, beating until just blended. Gather dough into a ball and enclose in waxed paper or plastic wrap; refrigerate several hours.

3. Preheat oven to 325° F. In a small saucepan combine cream and remaining 1 tablespoon sugar. Simmer over moderate heat until reduced by half; do not let cream boil over. Stir in pecans and set aside.

4. Divide dough into 42 pieces; roll each piece between your palms to form a ball. Place, 1½ inches apart, on greased baking sheets. Flatten cookies with the bottom of a glass dipped in sugar. Place approximately a teaspoon of pecan mixture atop each cookie.

5. Bake until lightly browned around edges (12 to 15 minutes). Transfer to wire racks to cool.

Makes about forty-two 1½-inch cookies.

CHOCOLATE-MINT SANDWICHES

Surround a thin chocolate mint with two warm chocolate wafers to make a luscious mint sandwich cookie.

- 1¾ cups sifted flour
- 2 teaspoons baking soda
- ¼ teaspoon salt
- ⅔ cup unsalted butter, softened
- ½ cup sugar
- 1 egg
- 1 teaspoon vanilla extract
- 6 ounces semisweet chocolate
- ¼ cup light corn syrup
- 48 thin, round, chocolate-covered mints

1. In a bowl sift together flour, baking soda, and salt; set aside.

2. In large mixer bowl cream butter until soft. Gradually add sugar and continue beating until light and fluffy. Beat in egg and vanilla.

3. Melt chocolate in top of a double boiler over hot but not simmering water. Add melted chocolate to butter mixture and beat thoroughly. Add corn syrup and beat until well combined. On lowest speed add flour mixture, blending until just combined. Gather dough into a ball and enclose in waxed paper; refrigerate several hours or overnight.

4. Preheat oven to 350° F. Work with one fourth of the dough at a time, keeping remainder in refrigerator. Divide each portion into 12 equal pieces. With your lightly floured hands, roll each piece into a small ball. Arrange balls, 2 inches apart, on ungreased baking sheets.

5. Bake until cookies feel slightly firm when touched gently (10 to 12 minutes). Remove from oven and let cookies stand on baking sheets for 1 minute. Then, one by one, make sandwiches. For each sandwich place a cookie upside down on wire rack; top with mint, then with another cookie right side up. Heat of cookies will melt mints slightly. Let stand on wire racks to cool completely. Store in an airtight container.

Makes about 4 dozen 2-inch cookies.

FINNISH CHESTNUT FINGERS

Chestnut purée colors and flavors these slender, finger-shaped cookies. Roll them generously in sugar before baking to give them a crunchy coating, then cool completely before serving to allow them to crisp.

- 6 tablespoons butter
- ¼ cup sugar
- 1 egg yolk
- ½ cup unsweetened chestnut purée, homemade or canned
- 1 teaspoon vanilla extract
- 1 cup flour
- ¼ teaspoon ground cinnamon
- ¼ teaspoon salt
- Sugar, for coating

1. In small bowl cream butter; gradually add the ¼ cup sugar and beat until light. Add egg yolk and beat well. Add chestnut purée and vanilla and blend thoroughly; set aside.

2. In a small bowl stir together flour, cinnamon, and salt. Gradually add to butter mixture, beating until just blended. Gather dough into a ball and enclose in plastic wrap or waxed paper; refrigerate several hours.

3. Preheat oven to 300° F. Work with one half of dough at a time, keeping remainder in refrigerator. Divide unrefrigerated dough into 15 pieces. On a lightly sugared work surface, roll each piece into a finger about 2½ inches long. Coat cookies generously with additional sugar. Repeat with other half of dough. Place cookies, about 1 inch apart, on greased and floured baking sheets.

4. Bake until cookies are lightly browned around edges (30 to 35 minutes); break one open to make sure it is done in center. Transfer to wire racks to cool.

Makes 30 cookies.

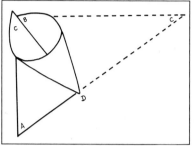

HOW TO MAKE A PAPER PIPING CONE

Cut square of parchment paper in half to form two triangles. (Use only one triangle.) Precut parchment triangles are also available in cookware stores. Take right-hand point (C) on longest side of triangle and fold in toward middle point (B) at top. Then take opposite point (A) and fold around until it also meets middle point (B) at top. The three points meet to form closed-tip (D) paper cone.

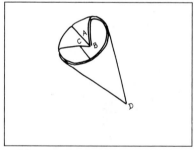

Fold point at open end of cone over toward closed tip of cone to prevent cone from unraveling.

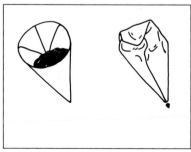

To use cone, fill no more than half full. Fold open end of piping cone down toward filling. Cut closed end of cone with scissors to form plain tube opening of size needed.

GINGERBREAD HOUSE

Young and old bakers alike are enchanted by the magic of a gingerbread house. If carefully cut and assembled, this one will keep for years stored in a cool, dry place. Instructions for assembling it are on page 112.

This recipe makes enough dough for one cake. Three cakes are needed to make the Gingerbread House pictured at left. The cakes are best baked separately. Do not try to double or triple the recipe; it is difficult to handle such a large quantity of dough. Since the cakes become firmer and easier to work with as they age, they are best baked at least a day before you assemble the house.

Royal icing is the edible glue that holds together the pieces of the house and adheres the candy decorations to the walls and roof. The icing is also used to outline the windows and doors. Because it is fast-drying, the icing is best made in three batches. It must be used quickly, before it forms a crust that clogs the tip of the pastry bag.

Be sure to have enough candies for decorating the house. The roof of the Gingerbread House took 13 to 16 ounces of multicolored candy wafers. Other decorations included gumdrops (10 to 11 ounces); transparent, multicolored, oval candy disks (7 to 8 ounces); bear-shaped jellied candies (5 to 6 ounces); 10 peppermint sticks; and sliced candy sticks with a design in the center (15 to 16 ounces).

Gingerbread

7½ cups sifted flour
1½ teaspoons baking soda
 1 teaspoon salt
 1 tablespoon ground cinnamon
 2 teaspoons ground ginger
 1 teaspoon each *ground nutmeg and ground cloves*
1½ cups vegetable shortening
1½ cups sugar
 1 bottle *(12 oz) light molasses*
 1 tablespoon vanilla extract
 1 tablespoon grated orange rind *(optional)*
    Candies, for decorating

Royal Icing II

 2 egg whites
 3 to 3½ cups confectioners' sugar

1. In a small bowl combine 1½ cups of the flour, baking soda, salt, cinnamon, ginger, nutmeg, and cloves; stir until thoroughly blended.

2. Preheat oven to 325° F. In mixer bowl combine shortening and sugar; beat until fluffy and well blended. Beat in molasses, vanilla, and orange rind (if used). Gradually add flour mixture, beating until well combined. Add remaining 6 cups flour, 1 cup at a time, mixing until well blended. When dough stiffens use a dough hook or knead until smooth.

3. Place dough in a greased, lightly floured, shallow-rimmed 10½- by 15½-inch baking pan, using your fingers to pat dough into place and press it into corners. With a rolling pin smooth out dough as evenly as possible.

4. Bake gingerbread until it pulls away from sides of pan and feels firm when touched lightly (about 35 minutes). Cool in pan on a wire rack for 5 minutes. While cake is still warm, cut out Gingerbread House pieces as described in steps 2 to 4 on page 112.

5. Repeat recipe 2 more times for enough gingerbread to make Gingerbread House. To assemble and decorate, see page 112.

Makes 1 cake (3 cakes required to make Gingerbread House).

Royal Icing II In a small bowl beat egg whites with electric mixer until stiff. Add sugar, ½ cup at a time, beating to incorporate completely after each addition. Continue beating at high speed for about 5 minutes or until icing is very stiff. Fit a pastry bag with a small star tip or other fluted tip; fill with icing (see page 99). Repeat recipe 2 more times as needed for enough icing to assemble and decorate Gingerbread House.

Makes about 1½ cups icing (3 batches required to make Gingerbread House).

This candy-trimmed Gingerbread House invites contemporary Hansels and Gretels to nibble while decorating the tabletop house with goodies.

111

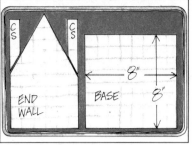

HOW TO ASSEMBLE THE GINGERBREAD HOUSE

Making the Gingerbread House pictured on pages 110–111 will be most enjoyable if the baking, assembling, and decorating are spread over several days, especially if children participate. Decorating the walls and roof is easiest when the pieces are laid out flat. To prepare the gingerbread and Royal Icing II for this Gingerbread House, see page 111.

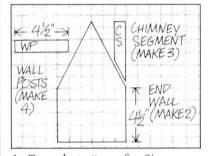

1. *To make patterns for Gingerbread House, use a ruler and pencil to draw a grid of 1-inch squares on cardboard. Draw patterns for end walls, chimney segments, and wall posts as shown above. You will also need patterns for base, front and back walls, and 2 roof pieces; refer to illustrations 2 to 4 for measurements. Use a ruler and sharp utility knife to cut out patterns.*

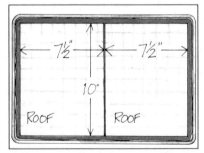

2. *Place cardboard patterns for 2 roof pieces slightly inside of baked edges of 1 still-warm cake. With a very sharp knife, cut gingerbread around patterns. (Cut carefully; pieces must fit together precisely to make a stable structure.) Remove patterns; leave cut gingerbread undisturbed until completely cool.*

3. *Slightly inside of baked edges of second still-warm cake, place patterns for base, 1 end wall, and 2 chimney segments. With sharp knife cut around patterns. Remove patterns; leave pan of cut gingerbread on wire rack until completely cool.*

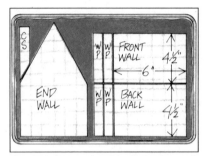

4. *Slightly inside of baked edges of third still-warm cake, place patterns for other end wall, front and back walls, 4 wall posts, and 1 chimney segment. With sharp knife cut gingerbread around patterns. Remove patterns; leave pan of cut gingerbread on wire rack until completely cool.*

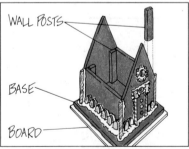

5. *With a metal spatula remove Gingerbread House pieces from pans and set on flat working surface. Prepare 1 batch of Royal Icing II (see page 111). Decorate front, back, and sides of house, piping on 1 row of icing at a time and*

pressing in candy decorations. Reproduce features of Gingerbread House pictured or invent your own. Allow icing on decorated pieces to dry (about 15 minutes). Set base of house on board. Prepare second batch of icing. Pipe onto bottom and adjoining edges of 1 end wall and back wall; press together to form corner and set on base. Hold in place a few minutes. Repeat with other end wall and front wall. Allow icing to dry (about 15 minutes). Pipe icing into inside corners; press wall posts into place as shown in drawing. Let stand undisturbed until icing is completely dry (at least 3 hours, or overnight).

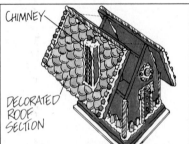

6. *Prepare third batch of icing. Pipe icing onto 1 side of each chimney segment. Sandwich together, making sure all edges are flush. Pipe icing onto bottom of assembled chimney and set on 1 side of roof; hold chimney in place a few minutes. Decorate roof by piping a thin line of icing along lower edge of 1 side of roof and pressing multicolored candy wafers into it (see photograph on pages 110–111). If necessary, cut wafers in half with sharp knife to fit. Repeat rows of icing and candy wafers until both sides of roof are covered. Pipe icing onto top edge of front wall and front slopes of end walls. Press 1 roof piece into position, placing it so other roof piece will meet it but not overlap at the peak. Hold in place a few minutes until icing is set. Pipe icing onto top edge of back wall and back slopes of end walls. Press other roof piece into position. Hold in place a few minutes until icing is set. Pipe icing into space between roof pieces. Attach additional candies to house by coating them with icing on one side and pressing them onto gingerbread.*

LEBKUCHEN

Lebkuchen (sacred cakes) are a boon to the holiday baker, because they can, and should, be made several weeks before Christmas. Let the dough rest at least a couple of days before baking to allow the spices to mellow. After baking, age the cookies at least two weeks to allow them to soften and improve in flavor. Germans bake their beloved *Lebkuchen* in a variety of shapes, including bars, rounds, and hearts.

    ¾ cup honey
    ¾ cup firmly packed brown
        sugar
    2 tablespoons unsalted butter
    1 egg, lightly beaten
    2 teaspoons powdered or
        granulated instant coffee
    ¾ cup finely ground almonds
    ¾ cup minced candied
        orange and lemon rind
    3½ cups sifted flour
    ½ teaspoon baking soda
    1 teaspoon ground cinnamon
    ½ teaspoon ground cloves
    ½ teaspoon ground cardamom

Confectioners' Sugar Glaze I

    ¾ cup sifted confectioners' sugar
    1½ tablespoons lemon juice

1. In a large saucepan combine honey, brown sugar, and butter. Cook over low heat, stirring constantly, until butter melts. Do not allow honey to boil. Set aside and let cool to room temperature.

2. Add egg and instant coffee to honey mixture; beat well. Beat in almonds and candied rinds; set aside.

3. In a bowl sift together flour, baking soda, cinnamon, cloves, and cardamom. Gradually add flour mixture to honey mixture, stirring with a wooden spoon. When mixture becomes too stiff to stir, turn it onto a lightly floured board and knead until smooth. Enclose dough in waxed paper or plastic wrap and refrigerate for at least 2 days or up to 5 days.

4. Preheat oven to 325° F. Divide dough in half; enclose half in waxed paper or plastic wrap and refrigerate. On a lightly floured surface, roll unrefrigerated dough into a 6-inch by 12-inch rectangle. Cut into twenty-four 3-inch by 1-inch bars. Place bars an inch apart on greased and floured baking sheets. Repeat with remaining dough.

5. Bake cookies until they feel firm when touched lightly (25 to 30 minutes). Transfer to wire racks; when barely warm, spread lightly with Confectioners' Sugar Glaze I.

Makes 4 dozen bars.

Confectioners' Sugar Glaze I In a small bowl combine sugar and lemon juice; stir until smooth.

BAD BOYS

Germans call these Christmas cookies *Spitzbuben* (bad boys), a name that belies their dainty appearance. Although most cooks use a similar dough, their methods of constructing the cookies differ. Some cut the dough with three graduated cutters, then sandwich them to make a three-tiered cookie. Others line a baking pan with most of the dough, then spread it with jam and top it with a lattice. The version below is a sandwich cookie; the top half has a hole in the middle to reveal the jam filling.

    1 cup unsalted butter, softened
    1 cup granulated sugar
    2 egg yolks
    ¼ teaspoon salt
    2¼ cups flour
    ⅔ cup (approximately) plum
        or lingonberry jam
        Confectioners' sugar,
        for dusting

1. In large mixer bowl cream butter; gradually add sugar and beat until very light. Add egg yolks, one at a time, beating well after each addition. Add salt, then gradually add flour, beating until just blended. Gather dough into a ball and enclose in waxed paper or plastic wrap; refrigerate for several hours.

2. Preheat oven to 350° F. Divide dough in half; roll half between 2 sheets of waxed paper to a thickness of ⅛ inch. Cut out rounds with a lightly floured, 2-inch-diameter cutter and transfer to ungreased baking sheets. Roll and cut other half of dough similarly, then cut a hole from the center of each round with a lightly floured thimble or ¾-inch-diameter cutter. Transfer rings to ungreased baking sheets. Reroll and cut scraps to form an equal number of rounds and rings.

3. Bake rounds and rings until lightly browned around edges (about 8 minutes). Transfer to wire racks. When cool, sift confectioners' sugar over rings. Spread a thin layer of jam on the top of each round and drop a dollop in the center. Working carefully, set a sugared ring over each round and press gently together.

Makes about 40 cookies.

Decorate buttery Spritz cookies before baking with your choice of candied fruits, colored sugars, silver balls, or multicolored sprinkles.

RASPBERRY-HAZELNUT BARS

Weave a lattice top on these nutty bar cookies to let the raspberry filling show through. They're pretty enough to grace a holiday tea table, yet sturdy enough to pack in a picnic or lunch box all year.

⅔ cup ground hazelnuts
½ cup butter or margarine, softened
½ cup firmly packed light brown sugar
¼ cup granulated sugar
½ teaspoon vanilla extract
1 egg
1 teaspoon grated lemon rind
1½ cups flour
½ teaspoon ground cinnamon
¼ teaspoon each *salt, ground nutmeg,* and *ground cloves*
¾ teaspoon baking powder
¾ cup red raspberry preserves
Confectioners' sugar, for dusting

1. Whirl hazelnuts in blender or food processor until powdery. In large mixer bowl cream butter, sugars, and vanilla until fluffy. Beat in egg until mixture is light colored. Mix in hazelnuts and lemon rind. Combine flour with cinnamon, salt, nutmeg, cloves, and baking powder; gradually add to butter mixture, beating slowly until combined. Enclose a third of the dough in plastic wrap and chill for about 30 minutes.

2. Preheat oven to 350° F. With your floured fingers, press remaining dough evenly over bottom of greased, 8-inch-square baking pan. Spread with preserves. Divide chilled dough into small pieces; roll pieces into strips long enough to cover preserves with a diagonal lattice pattern.

3. Bake until deep golden brown (30 to 35 minutes). Remove from oven and place on wire rack. While cookies are still warm, lightly sift confectioners' sugar over top. When cool, cut into bars about 1¼ inches by 1¾ inches.

Makes 2 dozen cookies.

SPRITZ

Buttery Spritz cookies are as much fun to make as they are to eat. With one easy dough and different plates in a cookie press, you can make wreaths, ribbons, rosettes, and other shapes. Before baking, dress up the shapes with decorating sugars or candied fruit, or flavor the dough itself with chocolate or ground almonds.

1 cup unsalted butter, softened
½ cup sugar
¼ teaspoon salt
1 teaspoon vanilla extract
1 egg
2½ cups (approximately) sifted flour

1. Preheat oven to 350° F. In large mixer bowl cream butter; gradually add sugar, beating until light. Add salt, vanilla, and egg; beat well.

2. Gradually add flour, beating until just blended. Dough should be firm—neither sticky nor stiff.

3. Transfer dough to cookie press and press dough onto ungreased baking sheets (see photographs at right). Bake until lightly browned around edges (about 10 minutes). Transfer to wire racks to cool. Store in airtight containers.

Makes about 8 dozen 1½-inch rosettes.

Chocolate Spritz Add 3 ounces melted and cooled semisweet chocolate to butter mixture; beat until blended. Increase flour to approximately 2¾ cups.

Toasted-Almond Spritz Use ½ teaspoon each vanilla extract and almond extract. Add ¾ cup finely ground, toasted almonds (see page 29) to butter mixture; beat until blended.

SPRITZ COOKIES

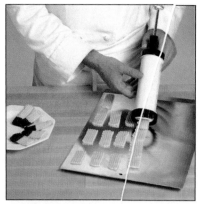

1. *To make ribbons use ridged plate. Form long strips, cut, separate slightly, and bake. When cool, dip into chocolate glaze of your choice.*

2. *Make rosettes with snowflake plate. Press candied cherry half in center of each cookie and bake.*

3. *Make wreaths with star plate. Form long strands; cut into 5-inch lengths. Shape into circles, decorate with silver balls, and bake.*

PECAN TASSIES

Use miniature muffin tins for these two-bite pecan pies, a holiday specialty in southern homes. Dark rum or bourbon gives a subtle kick to the filling, but the liquor can be replaced with a teaspoon of vanilla. Check hardware stores and cookware stores for tins with cups that measure about 1¾ inches across the top.

> 3 eggs
> 1 cup sugar
> 1 cup corn syrup
> 2 tablespoons unsalted butter, melted
> ¼ teaspoon salt
> ¼ cup dark rum or bourbon
> 1 cup minced pecans
> Melted butter, for greasing tins

Pastry Dough

> 3 cups flour
> 1 teaspoon salt
> ¾ cup chilled unsalted butter
> ½ cup vegetable shortening
> 6 tablespoons (approximately) ice water

1. In a medium bowl whisk together eggs, sugar, corn syrup, butter, salt, and rum until smooth and light. Whisk in pecans and set aside.

2. Preheat oven to 350° F. Brush cups and tops of tins with melted butter. On a lightly floured surface, roll out Pastry Dough to a thickness of not less than ⅛ inch. Cut out rounds with a lightly floured, 2½-inch-diameter cutter. Transfer to muffin tins; gently nestle into cups; patch any tears with extra dough.

3. Fill each pastry cup with a scant tablespoon of pecan mixture, stirring mixture occasionally to recombine. Bake until pastry is lightly browned (about 30 minutes). Let cool in tins for 2 minutes; carefully lift out tassies with a table knife and transfer to wire racks to finish cooling.

Makes about 5 dozen cookies.

Pastry Dough Combine flour and salt on a cool work surface. With a pastry blender or 2 knives, cut in butter and shortening until mixture resembles coarse crumbs. Add just enough ice water to make mixture hold together. Gather dough into a ball and enclose in waxed paper; refrigerate 30 minutes.

MINCEMEAT BARS

These quickly made bar cookies are dense, rich, and moist, thanks to a generous half cup of mincemeat in the batter. Although they keep well in an airtight container, they absorb their coat of powdered sugar; dust again with powdered sugar before serving.

> 2 tablespoons unsalted butter, melted
> ½ cup honey
> 2 eggs, lightly beaten
> ½ cup mincemeat
> ¾ cup chopped, toasted walnuts (see page 29)
> 1 cup flour
> ¼ teaspoon baking powder
> Pinch salt
> Sifted confectioners' sugar, for coating

1. Preheat oven to 350° F. In a medium bowl combine melted butter, honey, and eggs. Whisk well. With a wooden spoon stir in mincemeat and walnuts; set aside.

2. In a bowl sift together flour, baking powder, and salt. Add to mincemeat mixture and stir to blend.

3. Spread dough evenly in a greased 8-inch-square pan. Bake until cookies are lightly browned and feel firm when touched gently (about 25 minutes). Remove to a wire rack and let cool 10 minutes. Cut into sixteen 1-inch by 4-inch bars, trimming away uncut edges. While bars are still warm, drop into confectioners' sugar and roll to cover all sides generously. Finish cooling on wire rack. Store in an airtight container.

Makes 16 bars.

ITALIAN WAFER COOKIES

Italian Wafer Cookies *(cialde)* are a specialty of Montecatini, a Tuscan town noted for its curative waters and fashionable spa. These crisp, round anise wafers are sold in bakeries all over town; some bakers pack them in handsome, decorated tins. Made in a hot pizzelle or cialde iron, the cookies can be left in flat rounds or rolled into cylinders while hot. The irons are available in electric and stovetop models from cookware shops and well-stocked hardware stores.

> Vegetable oil, for pizzelle or cialde iron
> 2 eggs
> ½ cup sugar
> ¼ cup vegetable oil
> 1 teaspoon vanilla extract
> 1½ teaspoons anise seed
> 3 tablespoons brandy
> ⅓ cup water
> ¼ teaspoon salt
> ⅔ cup flour

1. Lightly brush grids of iron with vegetable oil; preheat iron according to the manufacturer's instructions.

2. In a large bowl whisk eggs and sugar until light; add oil and whisk until well blended. Add vanilla, anise seed, brandy, the water, and salt; blend well. Add flour and whisk until just blended.

3. When iron is hot, drop batter by tablespoons onto grids to make a neat, thin circle. (It is a good idea to make no more than 2 wafers at a time.) Close lid and bake until browned (45 to 60 seconds). (If you are using a stovetop iron, turn iron once or twice to be sure both sides of wafer are brown.)

4. Remove wafers from grids with a table knife and immediately use your fingers to roll each into a cylinder about 1 inch in diameter. Place cookies seam-side down on a wire rack until cool and crisp.

Makes about 2 dozen 4-inch cookies.

Anise-flavored Italian Wafer Cookies are made in a special pizzelle iron that makes a welcome gift for someone who loves to bake.

GERMAN FRUITED RUSKS

A spice dough studded with candied lemon rind and currants is shaped into long bars, then baked and sliced. Before slicing, dress the bars with a confectioners' sugar glaze and a sprinkling of colored decorating sugars. Serve with hot mulled wine or cider.

    2   cups sifted flour
    1   teaspoon baking powder
    ½   teaspoon baking soda
    ¼   teaspoon salt
    2   teaspoons ground cinnamon
    ¼   teaspoon ground cloves
    ¼   teaspoon ground cardamom
        or ginger
    3   eggs
    1   cup granulated sugar
    1½ teaspoons grated lemon rind
    ⅓   cup each dried currants and
        minced candied lemon rind
    1½ cups finely ground almonds
        Decorating sugars

Confectioners' Sugar Glaze II

    1   cup sifted confectioners' sugar
    ¼   teaspoon vanilla extract
    1½ tablespoons (approximately)
        milk

1. Preheat oven to 300° F. In a bowl sift together flour, baking powder, baking soda, salt, cinnamon, cloves, and cardamom. Set aside.

2. In large mixer bowl beat eggs with a whisk until light. Gradually add granulated sugar and continue beating several minutes until very thick and pale. Add lemon rind, currants, candied lemon rind, and almonds. Beat with a wooden spoon until well combined. Stir in flour mixture, beating until just blended.

3. Divide dough in thirds. On buttered and floured baking sheets—and using the back of a wet spoon to shake and smooth the dough—form dough into 3 logs each about 13 inches long by 2 inches wide by ¾ inch thick. Space logs well apart since they will spread during baking.

4. Bake until logs are lightly colored and feel firm when touched gently (about 25 minutes). Remove from oven and spread with Confectioners' Sugar Glaze II; immediately sprinkle with decorating sugars. Transfer logs to wire racks; let cool for 5 minutes. With a serrated knife cut logs crosswise into ¾-inch-wide slices. Let slices finish cooling on wire racks. Store in an airtight container.

Makes about 50 cookies.

Confectioners' Sugar Glaze II In a bowl combine sugar, vanilla, and just enough milk to make glaze smooth and spreadable. Mix well.

CHEWY CHRISTMAS MACAROONS

Mixed candied fruit gives these coconut macaroons a festive look. Be sure to beat the meringue well to dissolve the sugar and achieve good volume.

    4   egg whites, at room
        temperature
        Pinch salt
    1   cup sugar
    1   tablespoon lemon juice
    3   tablespoons flour
    3½ cups (about 10 oz) sweetened
        flaked coconut
    1   cup finely chopped, mixed
        candied fruit

1. Preheat oven to 275° F. In mixer bowl beat egg whites with salt to form peaks. Add ½ cup of the sugar, 1 tablespoon at a time. Add lemon juice, 1 teaspoon at a time. Beat 5 minutes at high speed; set aside.

2. In a bowl combine flour and remaining ½ cup sugar. Stir until well blended. Fold flour mixture into meringue; fold in coconut and all but 2 tablespoons candied fruit.

3. Drop mixture by rounded tablespoons, placed 1½ inches apart, onto greased and floured baking sheets. Garnish each cookie with some of the reserved candied fruit. Bake until cookies are lightly colored and feel firm when touched gently (about 30 minutes). Transfer to wire racks to cool. Store in airtight containers.

Makes about 3 dozen cookies.

COOKIES FOR OTHER HOLIDAYS

Around the world, special days are an excuse for special cookies. Some of these cookies, such as Hamantaschen (see page 122), recall an age-old legend. Others, such as *sfrappole* (see Italian Fried Sugar Wafers, below), have practical origins. Still others are merely intended as a festive addition to a holiday.

ITALIAN FRIED SUGAR WAFERS

Some Italians know these crisp cookies as *cenci* (rags), a name that suggests their sometimes irregular shape. Made from a pasta dough flavored with sweet white wine, the cookies can be cut into squares or ribbons or tied into knots before frying. After frying they are dusted with sugar and served hot with sweet wine or coffee. In Rome these fried wafers are known as *crespelle* or *sfrappole di carnevale* (carnival fritters) and are made to use up the fat in the days before Lent.

    2½ cups sifted flour
    ½   teaspoon salt
    2   tablespoons sugar
    2   eggs
    1   teaspoon vanilla extract
    2   tablespoons melted butter,
        slightly cooled
    ¼   cup sweet white wine or
        sweet sherry
        Salad oil, for deep-frying
        Vanilla Confectioners' Sugar
        (see page 39)

1. On a cool work surface sift together flour, salt, and sugar into a mound. Make a well in the center. Add eggs, vanilla, butter, and wine; mix with a fork to gradually incorporate flour. Finish mixing by hand; knead dough to form a smooth ball (3 to 4 minutes). Cover ball with a towel; let rest 1 hour in a cool place.

2. Divide dough in fourths. On a lightly floured surface, roll each part into a thin sheet about ⅛ inch thick and cut into ½-inch-wide strips. Tie each strip into a loose overhand knot.

3. In a large kettle or deep-fryer, heat at least 2 inches of oil to 375° F. Fry 2 or 3 cookies at a time, turning them over once when browned on the bottom. Total cooking time is less than a minute. Using a wire mesh spoon, transfer cookies to paper towels to drain. Sprinkle generously with Vanilla Confectioners' Sugar. Serve hot.

Makes about 56 cookies.

LINZER HEARTS

Cut these valentine cookies from a traditional *linzer* dough—a butter-rich Austrian pastry with ground hazelnuts. The dough is made in 5 minutes, and the cookies bake in 10. When cool, give the hearts a snowy coat of confectioners' sugar.

  1½ *cups sifted flour*
  ¾ *cup granulated sugar*
  ½ *teaspoon ground cinnamon*
     Pinch salt
     Grated rind of 1 lemon
  10 *tablespoons chilled unsalted butter, cut into pieces*
  2¼ *cups (approximately) finely ground hazelnuts*
  1 *egg yolk*
     Confectioners' sugar, for dusting

1. *To prepare in food processor:* In work bowl of food processor, combine flour, sugar, cinnamon, salt, and lemon rind. Process, using short on-off bursts. Add butter and process until mixture resembles fine crumbs. Transfer mixture to a large bowl; add hazelnuts and egg yolk and stir until well blended. Turn out onto a lightly floured board and knead briefly, just until mixture sticks together. *To prepare by hand:* In a large bowl stir together flour, sugar, cinnamon, salt, lemon rind, and hazelnuts. Turn mixture onto a cool work surface. With a pastry blender or 2 knives, cut in butter until mixture resembles fine crumbs. Add egg yolk and toss to blend. Knead briefly until mixture just sticks together.

2. Preheat oven to 375° F. Divide dough in half; enclose one half in waxed paper or plastic wrap and refrigerate. On a lightly floured surface, roll or pat unrefrigerated dough to a thickness of ¼ inch. Cut out cookies with a lightly floured, 2¼-inch, heart-shaped cutter. Transfer to ungreased baking sheets. Repeat with other half of dough.

3. Bake until lightly colored (about 10 minutes). Transfer to wire racks. When cookies are cool, sift confectioners' sugar over them. Store in an airtight container.

Makes about 4 dozen cookies.

Variation To make the valentine hearts pictured on pages 120 and 121, use a small, heart-shaped cutter to remove centers from half of the hearts cut in step 2. Bake large and small hearts and heart frames as directed. (Treat small hearts as miniature versions of above recipe.) When cool, lightly spread large hearts with raspberry jam. (You will need about ½ cup in all.) Sift confectioners' sugar on heart frames and set atop jam-spread hearts.

Makes 2 dozen cookies.

RUGELACH

Although Jewish delicatessens sell *Rugelach* throughout the year, these cream-cheese crescents are a Hanukkah tradition. They may be stuffed with nuts and raisins, as they are here, or with jam or poppy-seed filling if preferred. They do not keep well and should be eaten within a few hours of baking.

  ½ *cup raisins, coarsely chopped*
  1 *tablespoon brandy*
  1 *cup finely chopped, toasted walnuts (see page 29)*
  ½ *cup granulated sugar*
  1 *teaspoon cinnamon*
     Confectioners' sugar, for dusting

Cream-Cheese Pastry

  1 *package (8 oz) cream cheese, at room temperature*
  ½ *cup unsalted butter, at room temperature*
  ¼ *teaspoon salt*
  1 *tablespoon sugar*
  1 *teaspoon vanilla extract*
  1 *cup flour*

1. In a small bowl combine raisins and brandy; let stand 30 minutes. Add walnuts, sugar, and cinnamon; stir to blend.

2. Preheat oven to 425° F. Divide Cream-Cheese Pastry in half. On a lightly floured surface, roll each half into a thin round. With a sharp knife cut 10-inch-diameter circles from each round of dough by placing bottom of a 10-inch tart tin (or a 10-inch-diameter pattern cut from paper) on dough and cutting around it. Roll scraps from both circles into another thin round, and make an 8-inch-diameter circle by cutting around an 8-inch-diameter pattern cut from paper.

3. Sprinkle surface of each 10-inch circle with ⅔ cup raisin-nut filling; use ½ cup filling for 8-inch circle (a few tablespoons of filling will be left over). Press filling lightly with your hands to make it adhere to dough.

4. With a floured knife cut 10-inch circles into 12 wedges and cut 8-inch circles into 8 wedges. Starting with wide edge, roll each wedge toward tip, encasing filling. Arrange rolls on ungreased baking sheets. Place sheets in oven and immediately reduce heat to 400° F. Bake until lightly browned (12 to 14 minutes). Transfer to wire racks; when cool sprinkle with confectioners' sugar.

Makes 32 cookies.

Cream-Cheese Pastry In a bowl beat cream cheese, butter, salt, sugar, and vanilla until light and smooth. Add flour and beat until just blended. Gather dough into a ball and enclose in waxed paper or plastic wrap; refrigerate several hours or overnight.

Sandwich together plain and cutout Linzer Hearts (page 119) with raspberry jam to make a romantic offering for Valentine's Day.

GREEK EASTER COOKIES

At Easter, Greek bakeries are filled with crunchy *koulourakia* shaped into wreaths, pretzels, twists, fingers, or rings. Flavored with anise and sesame seed, these cookies are excellent for dunking in coffee or serving with an after-dinner brandy.

¼ cup sesame seed
½ cup unsalted butter, softened
½ cup sugar
2 eggs
1 teaspoon vanilla extract
1 teaspoon grated orange rind
2½ cups flour
2 teaspoons baking powder
¼ teaspoon salt
2 teaspoons anise seed
¼ cup brandy
  Whipping cream, for glazing
  Confectioners' sugar,
    for dusting

1. Toast sesame seed in a small skillet over moderately low heat, shaking skillet constantly, until seeds are lightly colored. Let cool.

2. In large mixer bowl cream butter; gradually add sugar and beat until light. Add eggs, one at a time, beating well after each addition. Beat in vanilla and orange rind; set aside.

3. In a medium bowl stir together flour, baking powder, salt, anise seed, and toasted sesame seed. Add to creamed mixture alternately with brandy. Beat until just blended. Gather dough into a ball and enclose in plastic wrap or waxed paper; refrigerate several hours.

4. Preheat oven to 400° F. Work with a third of the dough at a time, keeping remainder in refrigerator. Divide unrefrigerated dough into 12 pieces. On a lightly floured board, roll each piece into a rope about

¼ inch in diameter. Bring 2 ends of rope together. Hold 1 end of doubled rope in each hand and twist in opposite directions to form a spiral. Repeat with rest of dough.

5. Arrange spirals about 1½ inches apart on ungreased baking sheets. Brush lightly with cream. Bake until lightly browned (10 to 12 minutes). Transfer to wire racks; while cookies are still hot, sift confectioners' sugar over them. Leave on wire racks to cool completely.

Makes 3 dozen cookies.

HAMANTASCHEN

These three-sided Purim cookies recall the tricornered hat of Haman, an evil minister of the Persian Empire who tried to exterminate the Jews. The annual festival of Purim commemorates Haman's downfall and provides an excuse for eating poppy-seed–filled Hamantaschen.

⅔ cup unsalted butter, softened
½ cup sugar
2 eggs
1 teaspoon vanilla extract
3 tablespoons milk
3 cups sifted flour

Poppy-Seed Filling

½ cup poppy seed
¼ cup milk
¼ cup honey
¼ cup raisins
½ teaspoon grated lemon rind

1. In mixer bowl cream butter; gradually add sugar and beat until light. Add eggs, one at a time, beating well after each addition. Beat in vanilla and milk. Using lowest speed add flour, ½ cup at a time, mixing until just blended. Gather dough into a ball and enclose in waxed paper or plastic wrap; refrigerate at least 4 hours, or overnight.

2. Preheat oven to 375° F. Divide dough in half, keeping remainder in refrigerator. On a lightly floured surface, roll out unrefrigerated dough to

a thickness of about ⅛ inch, sprinkling with flour as necessary to keep dough from sticking. Cut dough into rounds with a lightly floured 2½-inch-diameter cutter.

3. Transfer rounds to ungreased baking sheets. Spoon a scant teaspoonful of Poppy-Seed Filling onto center of each round. Bring up sides of round and pinch together in 3 places to form a tricornered hat, leaving some filling visible in the center.

4. Bake until cookies are lightly browned around edges (about 12 minutes). Transfer to wire racks to cool. Serve warm.

Makes about 3 dozen cookies.

Poppy-Seed Filling Grind poppy seed in spice mill or blender until fine. In a small saucepan over low heat, stir together ground poppy seed, milk, honey, and raisins. Cook for 15 minutes, stirring occasionally at first, then frequently to keep mixture from sticking to pan. Mixture will thicken and pull away from sides of pan. Remove from heat and set aside; when cool stir in lemon rind.

CANDIED APPLE COOKIES

Delight little goblins at a Halloween party with fool-the-eye candied apples. These intriguing butter cookies are pierced with a toothpick while hot, dipped in caramel and nuts when cool, then nestled in miniature paper muffin cups.

   ½ *cup unsalted butter, softened*
   ⅓ *cup firmly packed brown*
      sugar
      Pinch salt
   ½ *teaspoon vanilla extract*
 1⅓ *cups flour*
  30 *light caramels*
   1 *can (5 oz) evaporated milk*
   1 *cup finely chopped,*
      toasted walnuts (see page 29)

1. In large mixer bowl cream butter; gradually add brown sugar and beat until light. Add salt and vanilla and beat until thoroughly blended. By hand, gradually add flour, stirring until well mixed.

2. Divide dough into 32 pieces, and roll each piece between your palms to form a ball. Place about 2 inches apart on ungreased baking sheets. Chill 30 minutes.

3. Preheat oven to 350° F. Bake cookies until lightly browned (12 to 15 minutes). Remove from oven and, while cookies are still hot, insert a toothpick in the top of each. Transfer to wire racks to cool.

4. In top of double boiler over simmering water, combine caramels and evaporated milk. Cook, stirring, until mixture is smooth. Place walnuts in a shallow bowl.

5. Dip cooled cookies into caramel mixture, letting excess drip off. Roll cookies in walnuts and set in miniature paper muffin cups.

Makes thirty-two 1¼-inch-diameter cookies.

Tiny, spherical cookies masquerade as taffy apples coated with caramel and chopped nuts, for a tricky Halloween treat.

INDEX

Note: Page numbers in italics refer to photos separated from recipe text.

U.S. MEASURE AND METRIC MEASURE CONVERSION CHART

		Formulas for Exact Measures				Rounded Measures for Quick Reference		
	Symbol	When you know:	Multiply by:	To find:				
Mass (Weight)	oz	ounces	28.35	grams	1 oz		= 30 g	
	lb	pounds	0.45	kilograms	4 oz		= 115 g	
	g	grams	0.035	ounces	8 oz		= 225 g	
	kg	kilograms	2.2	pounds	16 oz	= 1 lb	= 450 g	
					32 oz	= 2 lb	= 900 g	
					36 oz	= 2¼ lb	= 1,000 g (1 kg)	
Volume	tsp	teaspoons	5.0	milliliters	¼ tsp	= ¹⁄₂₄ oz	= 1 ml	
	tbsp	tablespoons	15.0	milliliters	½ tsp	= ¹⁄₁₂ oz	= 2 ml	
	fl oz	fluid ounces	29.57	milliliters	1 tsp	= ⅙ oz	= 5 ml	
	c	cups	0.24	liters	1 tbsp	= ½ oz	= 15 ml	
	pt	pints	0.47	liters	1 c	= 8 oz	= 250 ml	
	qt	quarts	0.95	liters	2 c (1 pt)	= 16 oz	= 500 ml	
	gal	gallons	3.785	liters	4 c (1 qt)	= 32 oz	= 1 l	
	ml	milliliters	0.034	fluid ounces	4 qt (1 gal)	= 128 oz	= 3¾ l	
Temperature	°F	Fahrenheit	5/9 (after subtracting 32)	Celsius	32° F	= 0° C		
					68° F	= 20° C		
	°C	Celsius	9/5 (then add 32)	Fahrenheit	212° F	= 100° C		